ON THE WALL WITH
SWORD AND TROWEL

The Challenges and Conflicts of Ministry

SANFORD ZENSEN

ON THE WALL WITH
SWORD AND TROWEL
The Challenges and Conflicts of Ministry

WIPF & STOCK · Eugene, Oregon

ON THE WALL WITH SWORD AND TROWEL
The Challenges and Conflicts of Ministry

Copyright © 2019 Sanford Zensen. All rights reserved. Except for brief quotations in critical publications or reviews, no part of this book may be reproduced in any manner without prior written permission from the publisher. Write: Permissions, Wipf and Stock Publishers, 199 W. 8th Ave., Suite 3, Eugene, OR 97401.

Wipf & Stock
An Imprint of Wipf and Stock Publishers
199 W. 8th Ave., Suite 3
Eugene, OR 97401

www.wipfandstock.com

PAPERBACK ISBN: 978-1-5326-9950-4
HARDCOVER ISBN: 978-1-5326-9951-1
EBOOK ISBN: 978-1-5326-9952-8

Manufactured in the U.S.A.

Scripture quotations taken from the New American Standard Bible® (NASB), Copyright © 1960, 1962, 1963, 1968, 1971, 1972, 1973, 1975, 1977, 1995 by The Lockman Foundation. Used by permission. www.Lockman.org.

Scripture quotations marked (NLT) are taken from the Holy Bible, New Living Translation, copyright ©1996, 2004, 2015 by Tyndale House Foundation. Used by permission of Tyndale House Publishers, Inc., Carol Stream, Illinois 60188. All rights reserved.

Scripture quotations marked (NIV) are taken from the Holy Bible, New International Version®, NIV®. Copyright © 1973, 1978, 1984, 2011 by Biblica, Inc.™ Used by permission of Zondervan. All rights reserved worldwide. www.zondervan.com The "NIV" and "New International Version" are trademarks registered in the United States Patent and Trademark Office by Inc.™

Scripture quotations taken from the Amplified® Bible (AMP), Copyright © 2015 by The Lockman Foundation. Used by permission. www.Lockman.org.

Scripture quotations marked "Phillips" are taken from The New Testament in Modern English, copyright 1958, 1959, 1960 J.B. Phillips and 1947, 1952, 1955, 1957, 1976 The MacMillan Company, New York. Used by permission. All rights reserved.

Unless otherwise indicated, all Scripture quotations are taken from THE MESSAGE, copyright © 1993, 1994, 1995, 1996, 2000, 2001, 2002 by Eugene H. Peterson. Used by permission of NavPress. All rights reserved. Represented by Tyndale House Publishers, Inc.

For Sharon who made the journey with me...

Contents

Introduction		xi
Chapter 1	THE GREATEST BATTLE OF ALL—FAITH	1
Chapter 2	THE DEEP DARKNESS—DOUBTS AND FEARS	17
Chapter 3	THE HEART OF THE MATTER—SIN	33
Chapter 4	THE REMEDY FOR BROKEN PEOPLE IN A BROKEN WORLD—GRACE	46
Chapter 5	THE TOUGHEST JOB OF ALL—MINISTRY	57
Chapter 6	THE ALTAR OF STRANGE SACRIFICE—MARRIAGE & FAMILY	71
Chapter 7	THE SEARCH FOR AUTHENTICITY—IDENTITY	82
Chapter 8	THE SURPRISE OF MINISTRY—JOY	98
Chapter 9	THE CALL TO DUTY & RESPONSIBILITY—THE CHARGE	113
NOTES		133

ABOUT THE AUTHOR

Sanford "Sandy" Zensen is an ordained Baptist and former Christian & Missionary Alliance minister with 20+ years' experience in the pastoral ministry. In addition, he has served 25 years as a Professor of Christian Studies and a Christian college administrator and continues to teach as an adjunct for two separate institutions. He holds two professional degrees, MDiv. (Gordon-Conwell Theological Seminary) and DMin. (Luther Rice Seminary) and a DPhil. in Religion and Society (Oxford/Omega Graduate School).

Sandy is a frequent speaker at churches, men's events, college alumni functions, and was the 2014 AGS (Adult and Graduate Studies) commencement speaker at Bryan College (TN). In 2017, he addressed the regional meeting of the Pastor-Theologian Project in Bangor, Maine, where he spoke on the topic, *"All the things they should have told me in seminary but didn't."* That presentation birthed the idea for his book, ON THE WALL WITH SWORD AND TROWEL. He continues to serve as a member and Sunday school teacher at Stuart Heights Baptist Church, one of the largest Southern Baptist churches in the Chattanooga, Tennessee area.

FOREWORD

Bill Johnson, PhD
Pittsfield, Maine

On the Wall with Sword and Trowel presents the principles of pastoral ministry Sandy Zensen taught me 40 years ago. Please permit me some autobiographical comments here for they serve to explain the thinking, passion, and experience behind the man who significantly influenced my life and ministry like no other.

I have enjoyed a rich and full career as a communicator. I am now a university professor, a seminary professor, a trainer of church planters, a teacher, and a pastor. I have been a pastor for decades. When I began, I did not know how to speak publicly, and when I did speak people either cringed or yawned. I had the privilege of coming under Sandy's "wing" when I was 23. He taught me how to *"correctly handle the Word of Truth"* (II Tim 2:15) and communicate it effectively and efficiently. Sandy was tough, firm, and fair. Like a good coach, he both encouraged and rebuked. What really drove me was the example of his own preaching and teaching. I came from a background where skillful pulpit speakers were rare, and though my pastoral education was well-intentioned, I had not seen many examples of effective ministry communication. When I first heard Sandy speak, I was mesmerized and captivated. Not only did he catch and hold my attention from start to finish, I found that his hearers recalled what he said. In fact, the points that he made from a biblical text, and the substance of his messages became the basis for our own conversations throughout the week. I remember meeting in the homes of our church members, and the default topic of conversation was invariably the sermon we had heard the previous Sunday and everyone seemed especially eager and waiting for the next message. We knew we would learn, be confronted with challenges from God's Word, and very likely hear the voice of the Holy Spirit speaking through His servant.

There was clearly natural, God-given talent in the man, as well as what one might refer to as a "charismatic" personality (in the older, non-religious sense of the word), but what made the greatest difference of all was his deep respect and awe for the Word of God. It simply could not be handled carelessly or without the reverence it deserved.

> *Thus says the LORD, 'Heaven is My throne and the earth is My footstool. Where then is a house you could build for Me? And where is a place that I may rest? For My hand made all these things. Thus all these things came into being, declares the LORD. But to this one I will look, To him who is humble and contrite of spirit, and who trembles at My word* (Isaiah 66:1-2, NASB).

Sandy was the first man I ever met who so obviously *"trembled"* at God's Word. He taught me to tremble as well, and that has made all the difference in my life and ministry. When I was examined in my preaching by my own denomination (The Christian Reformed Church) one of the comments that kept being repeated was how arrestingly authoritative my messages were. I believe if a man trembles before God and His Word and handles it accordingly, then the power of God behind His Word will confront the hearer: *"'Is not My word like fire' declares the LORD, 'and like a hammer which shatters a rock?'"* (Jeremiah 23:29, NASB). The preacher becomes a conduit through which the hearer comes in contact with the very word of God.

In the introduction to the book, the reader encounters sheer, stark realism as regards pastoral ministry. There is no attempt made to hide how difficult, demanding, and draining pastoral ministry can be. Make sure to read it. In *The*

Contemplative Pastor, Eugene Peterson notably described his approach to ministry at Christ Our King in Bel Air, Maryland. Similarly, Sandy does as Peterson did, explaining how he approached ministry and sought to mobilize the laity. This is a very interesting part of the book, and it sets the tone for what follows after. Unsurprisingly, it has some parallels with Peterson's thought.

The first chapter launches the reader into the fray of ministry. It is an honest and accurate portrayal of the conflicts, both spiritual and worldly, which are inescapably associated with the ministry. It reminds the reader of our need to resist evil in all of its guises. It is an honest account of a young man hurled into a conflict that he wasn't prepared for, and the story of his warfare.

The second chapter is perhaps the most powerful in the entire book. As a philosopher and an apologetics professor, I must say that no attack against the Christian faith is as hard to defend against as the attack on Christianity from the standpoint of the problem of evil, pain, and suffering. This chapter is not theodicy. One will find no nice neat formulas to explain why evil and suffering often seem so gratuitous in our all-good and all-powerful God's world. Sandy has captured the real-world anguish and pathos of ministry both honestly and poignantly. This material is practical as well as profound. It should be promoted at pastoral conferences. Sandy expresses his own doubts and fears which have beset him even as he sought to trust God in the midst of inexplicable suffering.

From there the book moves on to address the awfulness and pervasiveness of sin and all its outworking in "the real world." One is reminded of Dr. Karl Menninger's *Whatever Became of Sin?* in which the prominent doctor said that we need the biblical category of sin for practical reasons: there is simply no other word which will do to explain the awful things of which human beings are capable. This chapter is not for the faint of heart. As is only fitting, the next chapter addresses God's undeserved and unmerited kindness. It is a short and welcome respite from the weighty issues surrounding suffering and sin.

When I worked in ministry with Sandy, he used to like to quote a mutual acquaintance, a pastor who had left restaurant management in midlife in order to go into the pastoral ministry. That man (Frank) used to look at Sandy and say, "This is a rough business we're in brother." The rough business of pastoral ministry is artfully described in the fifth chapter. It deals frankly with the discouragement and bitterness with which ministers can often struggle.

I am known, both by my students and in our community, as a man who is devoted to family. I did not learn that lesson at home as a child. I might easily have sacrificed my family on the "altar of ministry," as so many have done. Having Sandy as my mentor when I was a young man was the single greatest factor that I can point to as to why I managed to keep my priorities in order across the years. The sixth chapter is his personal manifesto about the need to keep marriage and family uppermost in one's priorities whilst doing pastoral ministry.

Chapter seven focuses on the identity of the pastor. Quite simply it looks at whether one seeks identity and meaning in the esteem and respect of other human beings or in God. If one lives out the truth of God's call to ministry then there is an internal integrity, a wholeness, and a sense of vision and purpose which cannot be found elsewhere. The chapter is a call to find one's identity in God alone.

The eighth chapter engages the topic of joy. Interestingly, in the author's experience such personal joy has often been in the context of work outside of the church proper, where he served as a compelling witness for Christ in the local community. He found joy in the midst of the demands of ministry and offers a number of helpful, practical examples and insights to the reader. The necessity of balance is clearly depicted in the pages of this chapter. Years ago Sandy once told me that I needed to have a part of my life, whether within or outside the boundaries of the church, in which I was "winning." I have passed his advice on to the next generation of young pastors and church planters with whom I have worked.

So here you have a book by the one man who has most impacted my life for pastoral service and for the preparation and delivery of biblical messages. I have been to Bible college, seminary, and multiple graduate schools, but without detracting in any way from those fine institutions, I have learned more from the author you are about to read than I ever did from any of the schools I attended. Having read this book I can only say get ready to be made to think, to be exhorted, saddened, encouraged, taught, angered, to rejoice, to weep, to be reminded of truths you already know, to be stirred and motivated, to thank and praise God, and to wish for more.

The Charge, with which the book ends, was read to me, as I headed out to take the pastorate of a church on my own, having been Sandy's assistant for six years. Thirty-three years after having left that church, I still think of him as "my pastor" and still speak of him that way to our congregation here in Maine. I am incredibly grateful for Sandy's influence in my life, and if you will allow him to be, I know he will be a powerful influence for Jesus Christ in your life as well.

There is always more to knowing than human knowing will ever know. So the deepest knowledge can never be put into words—or spelled out in sermons, books, lectures, and seminars. It must be learned from the Master, under his authority, in experience.[1] ~ Os Guinness

INTRODUCTION

A few months into the pastorate convinced me that I was not adequately prepared for the pressures and strain of leading the local church. Consequently, I struggled, which is not an uncommon experience among pastors in all stages of ministry. One morning, only six months into the pastorate, I found myself sitting alone in my study feeling utterly despondent over the direction of the church and my own ineptness. I cried out to the Lord, *"If this is what pastoral ministry is all about, I'm not sure I can last 35 more years. It's going to take a better man than me."* And I wept.

Jon Ferguson, founding pastor of Christian Community Church (Chicago) told Christianity Today that if aspiring church leaders and pastors *"fully understood what ministry requires, they might not ever pursue it."*[2] My formal, professional training and seminary education had not equipped me to face the rigors of the pastorate or ministry in general. I'm not complaining, mind you. I had a quality, educational experience. I remember several of my professors warning a class of idealistic, energetic seminary students (of whom I was one), who wanted to change the world, about the daily routines and stresses associated with pastoring the local church, but I wasn't listening. Frankly, I had no real concept of what they were trying to say. I simply didn't get it. Nobody gets it, at least not until one walks through the doors of the church, attends a few disruptive, church business meetings, or stares into the swollen, red eyes of a distraught father who just learned that his precious son was killed in a car accident while traveling home. I wasn't ready for the onslaught of evil, which came in many forms.

Feeling called to serve the local church, Nik Ripken (later a missionary to Somalia) sought the counsel of an older pastor—whose candor surprised him. *"You don't want to become a preacher, Nik!"* the pastor said. *"Churches will eat you alive! That kind of work can kill a man!"*

Ripken later wrote, *"I was suddenly wondering, if in doing so (accepting God's call to serve) I had just condemned myself to hard labor and an unexciting life of misery."*[3]

I left seminary with what I thought was a solid theology, but theology, if it's worth anything at all, must be tested in the field of experience. Seminary gave me the "tools of the trade." I knew the principles of hermeneutics and how-to exegete a passage, put a sermon together, conduct a wedding, manage a funeral, and provide oversight to administrative meetings. I had the basics, but I lacked real world experience that no lecture could ever hope to provide. I needed more, if I was to survive and successfully handle the stress and strain of ministry.

Bruce Gerencser is a former pastor with twenty-five years of experience. He observed

> Young preachers begin the ministry with a lot of fervor and idealism. They go to their first church believing they are going to make a difference, that they are going to be able to do what others before them have not done… then the honeymoon period ends, and the preacher realizes that being a pastor is not what they thought it would be. Sometimes this is so devastating to the young preacher that they leave the ministry. The number of one and done pastors is quite high.[4]

I spent nearly twenty years in the pastorate serving four different, small town churches, none of which had more than 50–250 in attendance (average size of most American churches). Seminary taught me much, but not everything. No amount of professional training, personal counsel, or practical ministry (required in most M.Div. programs) could have adequately prepared me for what was to come. I had a lot to learn.

In talking with countless other pastors over the years, I've discovered that my experience was quite typical. One pastor noted,

> *I've had 8 1/2 years of somewhat formal theological education. In that time VERY LITTLE was practical church leadership/pastoral ministry. Of my 96 (credit) hours, less than 15 were of the practical pastoral subject matter. My earliest struggles in pastoral ministry were not in teaching, church strategy, etc., but in learning how to be a pastor and to love people. My pastoral ministry prof was a chaplain and taught the class from a heavy chaplaincy perspective. Had I not been a pastor's kid and had the benefit of 'seeing behind the veil' in my home growing up, I would have been absolutely clueless.*

No word more accurately describes my first few years in the pastorate than that—*"clueless."*

Preaching was one of the pastoral duties I most enjoyed. My own approach was expository in nature, starting at the beginning of a book or an epistle and working through to the end, verse by verse, chapter by chapter.

My first series of messages was rooted in Paul's letter to the church at Ephesus. I reached chapter four where the Apostle wrote that God had provided the church a variety of leaders—apostles, prophets, evangelists, pastors, and teachers *"for the equipping of the saints for the work of service, to the building up of the body of Christ"* (Eph 4:12, NASB) with the goal of establishing the *"unity of the faith"* and the maturing of the local assembly and its members (v. 13). The point was simply that each believer had a role to play in the life and ministry of the church. The concept was biblically sound, and I honestly thought that a few well-constructed sermons would quickly and dramatically change the long-standing practice of an ineffective church on the verge of closing its doors. I soon learned just how wrong I was.

Having laid out what I believed to be the biblical model, I informed the church that I couldn't (and *wouldn't*) do ministry alone—which was precisely the opposite of what this congregation (like so many) was accustomed to seeing. Much to the dismay of some church members, I insisted that each one find their place, roll up their sleeves, and get to work. The "dead," I reasoned, needed to rise, and walk. I was convinced that the laity must be involved, and my objective was to see that happen.

For starters, I insisted that laypeople prepare and print the weekly bulletin (if they wanted one), call the congregation to worship on a Sunday morning, fill the baptismal pool when needed, pray, read Scripture, make announcements during church services, etc., freeing me to focus on faithfully declaring the Word of God to the best of my ability. From the beginning, I attempted to train and prepare the church body for *"the work of service,"* encouraging, exhorting, and admonishing the saints to live out their faith at home, in the work place, and in the community. I saw that as my primary responsibility—and took it very seriously.

Three months into my ministry, following a Sunday morning service, I was standing at the front door of the church greeting people as they left the building. Because I was new to the church and the community, a deacon remained at my side to introduce me to those individuals I had not already met. The very first man out of the sanctuary (whom I later learned was quite influential) leaned in close and whispered in my ear, *"When are you going to grow up and be a man, and run this church by yourself?"*

I was stunned and responded, *"You apparently didn't hear a word I said in the last 30 minutes."* He turned and started out the door.

Sensing the tension, the deacon beside me immediately tried to smooth things over. He said, *"You better be careful, Al. The pastor is going to have you up there* (on the platform) *one of these days."*

To which the man shot back in anger, *"The hell he will!"* and marched out of the church. He never came back.

I sighed… and thought, *"Welcome to the pastoral ministry."* That was my first lesson. No doubt, there were *more* to come.

INTRODUCTION

The focus of this book is practical in every respect. The principles and observations are mine and grow out of my own personal and professional experience. I share them humbly in hopes of limiting the "surprise of ministry" for those (clergy and laity) who are called to the toughest of all divine assignments—serving the local church.

My prayer is that God might graciously use my story and the accompanying supplemental material to better prepare the ministry novice, encourage the veteran, and buildup followers of Christ, enabling each to "hang in there," fulfill their divine calling to service, and stay on the "wall" building and rebuilding the Kingdom of God for the glory of God. Like many before me, I quickly found that I needed a "trowel" in one hand and a "sword" in the other!

Yet, across the gulf of space... intellects fast and cool and unsympathetic, regarded this earth with envious eyes, and slowly and surely drew their plans against us.[1]
~ H.G. Wells, *War of the Worlds*

CHAPTER 1

THE GREATEST BATTLE OF ALL—FAITH

Little did I know that the pastorate would take me to the front-lines in the greatest cosmic battle of all—the fight for the souls of men and women and my own spiritual survival. It is indeed a "War of the Worlds."

As a young pastor, I found myself in a war zone at my first church trustee meeting. The board had decided to have the sanctuary of the church repainted. The bid came in at $2100 for the project. So, to avoid having to go to the church for final approval, the board opted to pay the contractor in three payments of $700 and thus bypass the congregation. This action would be a clear violation of the church's by-laws which stated that any indebtedness above $700 would require a duly called business meeting. I interrupted the meeting and informed the board that we must adhere to our own constitution and governing policy and that we should not and cannot proceed further in this manner. Though I did not say it, I felt strongly that the plan was deceptive, dishonest, and certainly disrespectful toward the church body. Much of the board vehemently disagreed, and I found myself in a fight. I held my ground and didn't back down. In fact, I went on the offensive and warned the board that, should they ignore or reject my counsel and insist on moving forward with this project without calling a business meeting of the church, I would stand in the pulpit on Sunday morning and inform the congregation. Furthermore, I advised them that they could be held financially responsible to pay the contractors for work completed should the church vote against the project. Tensions ran high.

The next afternoon while I was away on a pastoral call, the chairman of the board showed up at my house yelling at my wife, *"Who the hell does that young pastor think he is coming in here and telling us what we can and cannot do?"* She didn't respond to the attack but quietly and graciously informed the man that I was not in my office and closed the door. I never imagined that such a battle over "doing right" would ever have to be fought within the context of the church. I was naïve.

Ron Walters, who wrote monthly letters to 50,000 pastors and church leaders, reminded them (as if they didn't already know) that

> Despite its public persona, pastoring is filled with stress. It's an ecclesiastical toxin that saps your energy; a stubborn pimple on the face of the church; a mental battering ram that beats on your office door. At times it's the enemy standing on the other side, but sometimes it's your sheep. Either way, it's a workplace staple and the single biggest drain to a pastor's personal joy.[2]

The stress is inevitable. In just a few verses (Ephesians 6:10–12), the word *"against"* (pros) is repeated five times by the Apostle Paul, as a reminder to the church, to *"stand firm"* in the faith in the most trying of conflicts, opposing the onslaught of the kingdom of darkness. Détente is not an option in this great battle.

Spiritual conflict is all too real in this world, and the pastor, ministry leader, and any follower of Christ desiring to serve the interests of His kingdom will most certainly be in the thick of the fight. There is no escape. On every street corner in the community, including within the walls of the local church, God's man or woman will be under fire, living, serving, and fighting against the *"strategies of the devil… against evil rulers and authorities of the unseen world, against mighty powers in this dark world, and against evil spirits in the heavenly places"* (Eph. 6:10–12, NLT). The pastor may very well find his pulpit riddled with "bullet holes." I did. After all, "shots" were fired nearly every Sunday morning.

It is a battle for which I was unprepared. It is one thing to know of the enemy. It is quite another matter to experience his destructive intent firsthand, to feel his cold, angry glare of disdain and hatred, and to see the horrors of evil upfront and personal. Evil unmasked is a terrible sight for any man or woman to see.

The eight-volume encyclopedia, *Social Issues in America,* identifies a variety of disturbing and destructive health and behavioral issues. The problems, familiar to every pastor and ministry leader, included (among other things) AIDS/HIV, alcohol abuse, anti-semitism, cancer, academic cheating, civil rights and liberties, child abuse and molestation, divorce and child support, euthanasia, hate-crimes, heart disease, homelessness, media sex violence, obesity, pornography, rape, rioting, racism, suicide, etc.[3] The *New York Times* recently reported that suicide rates among middle age Americans have risen dramatically in the last thirty years,[4] including a 10-year increase in suicide for middle school students.[5] More than once during my pastoral ministry I have wept over the grave of a suicide victim. The pain is deep for the surviving families and the funerals are some of the toughest to oversee. Obviously, the battle rages on numerous fronts and many families and individuals are left wounded, hopeless, and despairing. There is no shortage of social ills to combat. The wounded lay everywhere.

Sharon Watkins, the General Minister and President of the Christian Church (Disciples of Christ) in the United States and Canada, prayed *"that we all will find the courage to face the truth* (about what is going on in our communities and churches) *and do something about it."*[6] While the pastor is generally expected to lead the "troops" into battle to *"do something,"* he or she is ill-prepared and ill-equipped for the rigors of the battlefield. Training with *"divinely powerful"* spiritual *"weapons"* (II Corinthians 10:4) that require the exercising of a relentless, ruthless faith does not necessarily happen in an academic setting void of real-world experiences.

The pastorate forced me to face reality: broken marriages, dysfunctional families, neglectful parents, abused children, rebellious teenagers, poverty, racial prejudice, disease, death, drugs and alcohol addictions, desperate people wandering the streets homeless and alone, the occult, forgotten and forsaken older adults—so much pain. When human tragedy dismantles and destroys life as God intended it to be lived, the church ought to be there on the front lines bringing the power, grace, and mercy of God to the fight—not hiding away behind the four walls of a pristine building, singing hymns and lighting candles. There amid all that suffering is where Christ's church must be found—clothed in battle array, the armor of God; aggressive, militant, destroying the *"fortresses of demons"* and the works of the Devil. The need for an effective, spiritual battle-plan with a strong faith to take on such destructive and powerful enemies of the human soul is often missing from formal educational demands and theological preparation. Though lectures, books, and research are all critical and essential for intellectual training, the "fight" is much more than an academic exercise.

One quiet afternoon two 13-year old girls were playing with a Ouija Board, when one of them without warning threw her friend to the ground and started choking her. Both hands were wrapped tightly around the girl's thin neck. She was gasping for air and fighting for her life. Her mother heard the commotion, ran into the bedroom, and rescued her daughter. Desperate for answers, the mother called to inform me of the incident and asked what she needed to do. I made a quick mental sweep through my seminary notes and found little to deal specifically with the unleashing of Hell's fury. I was scared and did the only thing I knew how to do—pray frantically for God's protection and direction, which He gave, and a young girl was rescued, and peace restored to the family.

THE GREATEST BATTLE OF ALL—FAITH

Ministry often felt like I was in the middle of a great war—actually, I was. When seminary ended, I discovered the "fine print" written on the Master of Divinity degree now hanging on my office wall. It included God's orders *"with all the rights and privileges appertaining to"*—orders that sent me to the front lines of the battle. They were as clear as Winston Churchill's warning to the English people during World War II. His words are profoundly applicable to the church.

He promised that following the war London would be rebuilt *"more beautiful than before"*, but prior to that day, he cautioned

> *Long dark months of trials and tribulations lie before us. Not only great in danger, but many more misfortunes, many shortcomings, many mistakes, many disappointments will be our lot. Death and sorrow will be the companions of our journey; hardship our garment; constancy and valor our only shield.*[7]

The Scriptures give ample evidence to the reality of the fight. Moses battled the power of Egypt. He fought blatant idolatry within his own ranks and stood toe-to-toe against an army of Amalekites who were hell-bent on stopping the advancement of God's people. Joseph fought off Potiphar's wife. Joshua strapped on armor to tear down the walls of Jericho and march to take the land of Canaan promised by God to Israel. Caleb conquered mountains. Gideon pulled down the altar of Baal. Nehemiah faced down his critics and battled to rebuild the walls of Jerusalem. Elijah fought with the pagans of his day. David struck a lethal blow with a sling and a stone and brought down a giant named Goliath. Esther fought hatred, prejudice, and persecution. John the Baptist battled the immorality of a king. Jesus took on religious leaders who oppressed the people and stood in opposition to God's word. He called them *"hypocrites"* and *"snakes"*—fighting words, if you ask me. The disciples were ready to *"strike with the sword,"* when the mob arrived at Gethsemane to arrest Jesus. Throughout his entire ministry career, Paul fought to maintain doctrinal purity and rid the early church of false teachers. Peter refused to be silent in declaring Christ crucified and insisted on the need for repentance (Acts 2:38). Stephen battled false charges and defended the Gospel with his life. The "battle" is no stranger to those who would serve under the banner of the Cross.

My first real confrontation with the "enemy" occurred shortly after I arrived at a church to assume pastoral leadership. I made a hospital visit to an elderly couple who had been married for more than fifty years. They shared a hospital room, both having been admitted for some medical condition. While I was there, the husband went into cardiac arrest and "all hell broke loose." His monitor went haywire. The alerts sounded, and the medical staff rushed down the hallway and into the room with the "crash cart." The man's wife panicked and started screaming. It was pure chaos. I froze, unsure of what to do next. In an instant, my mind raced through eight years of undergraduate and graduate education and classroom notes, looking for an answer, but found none. Nothing could have prepared me for this. I felt so inadequate, powerless, and confused, and frankly, I was. I did not know how to "fight." Amid the bedlam a thought came to me. It was a "battleplan" to face down the onslaught of man's cruelest enemy—death. It was simply this: *"Open the Word and read. Unsheathe that Sword and wield it."* And so, I did. In a quiet voice, I released in faith the power of God's Word.

> *I will lift up my eyes to the mountains;*
> *From whence shall my help come?*
> *My help comes from the Lord,*
> *Who made heaven and earth,*
> *He will not allow your foot to slip;*
> *He who keeps you will not slumber…*
> *The Lord will protect you from all evil;*
> *He will keep your soul.*
> *The Lord will guard your going out and your coming in*
> *From this time forth and forever* (Psalm 121, NASB).

Before I could finish reading the psalm, peace mercifully descended upon that chaotic room and the people in it. Immediately, everything settled, and calmness returned. God had shown up for the battle and His Word prevailed. Though the man later died, desperation and despair were replaced with faith and courage, and the hopelessness of death was beaten back—a lesson well learned.

Not knowing or understanding what was to come in the years ahead, I selected a song written in 1529 by Martin Luther for my ordination service. It has been called the "Battle Hymn of the Reformation"—*A Mighty Fortress is Our God*. The words of that great hymn proved prophetic for my ministry. In hearing them that day, I got the sense that I was about to step onto a "battleground" filled with *"devils… (who) threaten to undo us."* I would find them everywhere, disrupting and destroying lives at every opportunity. I often felt helpless, hapless, and hopeless in this relentless struggle against *"our ancient foe," "the Prince of Darkness,"* whose *"craft and power are great."* The futility of relying on my *"own strength"* to fix all that had gone wrong in the lives of the people I served became painfully apparent. I needed something more. Later, I would learn the need for that *"one little word,"* the truth of God's word and the *"right Man on our (my) side,"* if I ever hoped to take the fight to the enemy of our soul and see the results I was after. I required balance between the reality of evil with its intent on destruction and mayhem and the power of God to bring *"triumph"* in Christ Jesus. God alone, I realized, would *"win the battle."* The second verse of the hymn puts things in clear perspective:

> *Did we in our own strength confide, our striving would be losing;*
> *Were not the right Man on our side, the Man of God's own choosing:*
> *Dost ask who that may be? Christ Jesus, it is He;*
> *Lord Sabaoth, His Name, from age to age the same,*
> *And He must win the battle.*[8]

I needed that sort of faith, faith in God and faith in His word—something I would have to learn by experience on the field.

John Wesley knew of the battle. A page from his diary reads as follows:

Sunday morning, May 5, preached in St. Ann's, was asked not to come back anymore. Sunday p.m., May 5, preached at St. John's, deacons said, "Get out and stay out." Sunday a.m., May 12, preached at St. Jude's, can't go back there either. Sunday p.m., May 12, preached at St. George's, kicked out again. Sunday a.m., May 19, preached at St. somebody else's, deacons called special meeting and said I couldn't return. Sunday p.m., May 19, preached on the street, kicked off the street. Sunday a.m., May 26, preached in meadow, chased out of meadow as a bull was turned loose during the services. Sunday a.m., June 2, preached out at the edge of town, kicked off the highway. Sunday p.m., June 2, afternoon service, preached in a pasture, 10,000 people came to hear me.[9]

Now, that's a good fight by any standard, coupled with a tenacious faith that would not give-up or give-in to discouragement and disappointment. No one acquires perseverance of faith in the safety of a schoolroom. You learn that in the thick of the "fight." It is there in those difficult moments that one discovers the sufficiency of Christ and His word to see you through the most troubling of times. That experience strengthens spiritual resolve and enlarges faith, a lethal combination to take into battle.

Many years ago following seminary graduation a friend told me the true story of a first-year pastor (he knew personally) who was having a good deal of trouble in his ministry. So, the young pastor called his father to ask his advice and grumble about the considerable difficulties and heartaches he was experiencing while trying to lead his church. His father listened for a bit and then abruptly stopped his son and interrupted his complaining. He asked him a simple, yet profound question:

"Son, do you believe that Jesus does all things well?"

And his son responded, *"Why, of course, Dad. I do!"*

His dad shouted back, *"Good!"* and hung up the phone! Discussion over! Nothing more really needed to be said. The father's message? Trust God. There are no other viable options.

The lesson was clear. The size of my faith mattered little. I didn't have much anyway. Of greater importance in ministry (and daily life) was the size of the God in whom I placed my trust. That lesson would be reinforced again and again through the years until it penetrated the thick skull of "ole bonehead" (that's me).

I will not ever forget the first time I met Daniel, a young man from Nigeria. I had picked him up at the airport, and immediately engaged him in conversation. I asked, *"What does your father do for a living?"*

He said, *"He's a pastor."*

I responded, *"Great! How big is his church?"*—a typical question from a rationalistic, western perspective.

Daniel replied, *"Six."*

I thought I had misunderstood, so I ask for further clarification. *"You mean sixty? Six hundred?"*

He said, *"No, six."*

So, I asked (another stupid question), *"How does your father manage to put food on the table? How does he take care of the family?"*

He looked at me as if he couldn't believe what he had just heard, surprised that I didn't already know the answer. He was stunned, maybe a bit disappointed. After all, I was supposed to be a believer with a decade or more of pastoral experience behind me.

He paused for a moment, turned toward me, and simply said (as if I should have known), *"God! My father taught me to walk by faith and not by sight. And I wouldn't want it any other way."*

At that moment, I felt as if I had the spiritual IQ of a plant. I had foolishly forgotten to calculate God into the equation of everyday life.

Daniel's father understood the character and role of faith in ministry. He walked by faith. He lived by faith, and his son was fully convinced that God would supply His needs, and He did—a much needed lesson for me to learn, if I was to advance the cause of Christ in a significant way.

A 3-year-old girl was the victim of child abuse while enrolled at a church pre-school. Nineteen years later the full impact of that experience hit with a vengeance. Guilt and self-condemnation engulfed her. She felt helpless, without hope, alone, crippled by fear and crushed under the weight of a demoralizing depression. Consequently, the young woman attempted suicide several times. She penned the following words. It was a plea for help from anyone who might take up her cause and rescue her from the battle:

Does anyone love me?
Does anyone care?
Can't anyone realize?
Or see the pain that is there?
Is there such a thing as a true friend?
One who will stand by me,
Be there till the end?
Everyone who listens says,
"I'll keep you in prayer!"
They pray for others to help
But refuse to be there!
Is that what I'm to expect
For the rest of my life?
No one to carry my burdens?
No one to comfort my strife?

I helplessly watched the agony of that young woman with little understanding of what to do to ease her pain and heal her wounded heart. I had my doubts and a multitude of fears. Life was simply out of control, more importantly, out of my control. The problem was big, but my faith was smaller still. Like the disciples of old, I had *"so little"* of it (cf Matt. 17:20, NASB), which proved problematic until I discovered that a *"little"* faith was enough. In fact, faith the size of *"a mustard seed"* was all that was required, a simple reliance upon a great, big God that could and would step in to redeem the situation. In the end, He did just that and I learned faith on my knees pleading for her life and for the well-being and restoration of her soul. I firmly anchored my mind and heart to the God of the Bible, and I was not disappointed. My faith, what little there was of it, rested on the One who holds the oceans in *"the hollow of His hand,"* and measures the vast universe by the span of His fingers (Isaiah 40:12, NASB). Though the scars from early childhood abuse remain to this day, God used the tragedy in her life to develop the necessary personal and professional skills and compassion to serve and help others recover from their own pain and brokenness. *"I do believe; help my unbelief"* (Mark 9:24, NASB).

I shamefully admit that I lacked the spiritual maturity and fortitude to effectively and successfully *"fight the good fight of faith"* (I Tim. 6:12, NASB). Yet, that is precisely what the church is called to do—to get in the fight, engage the Enemy on every front, *"Rescue the perishing… (and) lift up the fallen."*[10]

Where is the church that has *"turned the world upside down?"* Where is the church that sounds the strong, rhythmic beat of Heaven's war drums? Regrettably, the old hymn, *Onward Christian Soldiers,* has been removed from some church hymnals. It was thought to be antiquated and violent, yet it arguably remains the marching orders of the church to advance deep into a world void of the Gospel and bring to bear the mercy and love of God. Sabin Baring-Gould originally wrote that song to be used during a festival for *"children to sing when marching from one village to another."*[11]

Onward, Christian soldiers,
Marching as to war,

With the cross of Jesus
Going on before.
Christ, the royal Master,
Leads against the foe;
Forward into battle
See His banners go!

Where is the church that will take up arms for those poor in body and spirit—desperately in need of mercy and compassion? Where is the church, empowered by the Holy Spirit, to give sight to the blind and guidance to those who have lost their way? Where is the church that will boldly enter the dark prisons of human fear and despair with deliberate intent to remove the burdensome chains of despondency and discouragement, and set people free? Where is the church that will seize the lame—the physical, emotional, and spiritual cripples of this world, and say, in the power of God, *"I do not possess silver and gold, but what I do have, I give to you. In the name of Jesus Christ, the Nazarene—WALK"* (Acts 3:6, NASB)! The world needs a church like that and the church needs pastors, ministry leaders and disciples like that. Such fervency and focus are desperately needed in today's ministry to the multitudes of men and women struggling to rise up and live life fully— a fact often lost amid language studies, term papers, and final exams.

At West Point, there is a monument near the center of campus to honor General Douglas MacArthur. I recall standing reverently and quietly in the middle of those grey granite and marble walls that encircled me, feeling like my feet stood solidly on hallowed ground.

I began reading a portion of *MacArthur's final address to the Corp*, delivered on May 12, 1962, and carved in the surrounding rock. I circled ever so slowly, so I could fully take in the power of those marvelous words. They deeply moved me. It did so then; it does so now.

It reads:

Your mission remains fixed,
Determined, inviolable –
It is to win our wars…
Yours is the profession of arms –
The will to win.
The sure knowledge that in war
There is no substitute for victory.

I was not prepared for the harsh reality of this great, cosmic battle for the cause of Christ and for the redemption of those within the church and on the streets of the local community. There is no getting around it. I was forced to take up *"sword"* and *"shield"* and face the conflict to survive, but first I needed the *"will to win"* and to learn a great lesson—In war, *"There is no substitute for victory."*

This *War of the Worlds* is more than conceptual. The fight is real. The casualties are real. The enemy is real. Yet, there is no need to be *"afraid"* or *"discouraged."* The *"battle,"* from start to finish, was not mine *or "yours"* anyway. The battle, ultimately and always, belongs to God (cf II Chronicles 20:15, TLT).

THE WARRIOR'S CODE

"Finally, be strong in the Lord." (Eph 6:10, NASB)

At last,
Divine orders to toughen-up,
For the Enemy waits.
The Devil.
Wicked.
Vile.
Hateful.

Striking.
Scheming.
To disillusion,
Disorient,
Discourage.
And ultimately,
To destroy
the likeness and work of Christ in me.

Shall I quit the battle?
Whipped.
Wounded.
Whining.
A vanquished saint?
A hapless victim?
Or
Shall I live and die as victor,
More than a conqueror?

Onward
Christian soldier!
The **WARRIOR'S CODE.**
The battle cry.
"Stand firm!
No surrender… EVER!"

Quickly,
On with the armor of God,
The Captain's command,
In FULL battle array,

The Spirit's Sword in hand.
Strike down
every thought raised up against the knowledge of God.
Scale the fortresses of demons
wherever found.
Retake the land.
Make it, again,
Holy Ground.

Forward,
With a warrior's heart.
In the strength of His might,
Fight!
Under the banner of Heaven's Sovereignty,
Power and authority.
In the name of the King,
Christ Jesus,
The Lord God Almighty.

Advance!
For Him.
With Him.
In Him.
Standing orders for all soldiers of the Cross.
Subdue the Adversary.
Subjugate his armies.
Seize his possessions.
Enlarge Heaven's dominion everywhere.

Arise!

To challenge,
To conquer,
To change.
Sacredly endowed.
Spiritually enthroned.
Sufficiently equipped.
"Having nothing, yet possessing everything" for triumph:
   The indomitable Spirit to overcome,
   The stubborn will to win.
   The gritty guts to "fight the good fight" to the last,
   The audacity to dare to "hope against all hope."
   The faith to believe God can.
   The nerve to decide God will.

First.
Last.
Always.
"Be strong in the Lord!"
Stand firm!
Be on the alert with all perseverance."
The battle wages on
'til the final trumpet!

   ~ Sandy

Where is God?... go to Him when your need is desperable, when all other help is vain, and what do you find? A door slammed in your face, and a sound of bolting and double-bolting on the inside. After that, silence... the conclusion I dread is not 'so there's no God after all,' but 'so this is what God's really like. Deceive yourself no longer.[1] ~ C.S. Lewis

CHAPTER 2

THE DEEP DARKNESS—DOUBTS AND FEARS

Having completed my theological studies, I stood in line, dressed in cap and gown, waiting for the commencement exercises to begin. I had worked hard over the previous three years and for a brief moment, I felt a tinge of pride and excitement. Now I was about to be rewarded for my efforts—a seminary degree, something I once thought was out of reach. Prior to the start of the ceremony, I carefully considered the prospects of my future ministry, took an honest, hard look at my current strengths and abilities, and realized just how little I knew, how unprepared I was to go out into the field and serve as pastor of a local church. I felt like I knew nothing of any real substance, and frankly at that moment, I was unaware of just how right I was. A good education might very well do just that. My knowledge of the big issues of life, death, and eternity, and where God and genuine faith fit into a world filled with tragedy and heartbreak was seriously lacking. Experience, I discovered, is a much more effective teacher than a seminary degree, though both are needed.

Some things happen in life that defy explanation and understanding. For example, in the movie, *Remember the Titans*, the team had lost its star defensive player (a two-time High School All-American) to a tragic car accident that left him paralyzed from the waist down. The event took place just before the Virginia state championship game. His entire future was turned upside down and a brilliant, future football career would be no more. He was devastated, and the team was distraught. In discussing the tragic circumstances, Coach Boone's wife attempted to get a handle on what had just happen. She tried to console her husband and soothe his aching heart. She made this observation: *"Sometimes life is hard for no apparent reason."* I couldn't agree more. Every pastor and ministry leader will face that reality in the lives of his or her parishioners and in his or her own life. Some things happen in life that defy explanation and understanding.

One night I got up about 1:00 AM, quite restless and unable to fall back to sleep. Within a few minutes, the phone rang. Phone calls at that time of night are usually not good, and this was no exception.

"Hello. Is this the Zensen household?"

"Yes."

"Is this the son-in-law of Irene Gage?"

'Yes. May I help you?"

"This is Irene's next-door neighbor. There's been a fire. The entire house was engulfed in flames. The firemen climbed in the back window of the only part of the house that was still standing. They tripped over her body lying on the floor. She was alive, but severely injured, and they've taken Irene to the burn unit in Westchester County. I just wanted to let you know."

I thanked her for calling. Hung up the phone and got my wife up to tell her the news. We were both in shock, disbelieving what we had just heard. The next morning, we were on an early flight headed for upstate New York.

We went directly to the hospital. Eleven days later, Irene died from first and second-degree burns, and respiratory damage caused by extensive, smoke inhalation. It was horrible. Irene was in her late eighties, living alone on a back, country road, when lightning struck the house and set the place ablaze. The state fire marshal called it an *"act of God."* I was there for the evaluation.

THE DEEP DARKNESS—DOUBTS AND FEARS

I couldn't get my head around those words and the resulting tragedy. How could this happen? Why did it happen? Was God responsible for this? What possible purpose could this serve? What good could come of it? I didn't see it. I had no ready answers (still don't), and I was angry with God—the God of whom it is said, *"has a wonderful plan for my life."* I didn't buy it—not then.

Dave and Irene Gage were wonderful people. They spent their entire lives together serving the interests of the Kingdom of God. They were a team. Dave was a church planter, pastor, and school teacher, ministering to the people of his community. Irene worked at his side, served with Child Evangelism Fellowship, and in her later years, she was a mentor to younger women and brought comfort and encouragement to those confined to a nursing home.

I thought, *"God, they were kind, gentle people, who served You all of their lives? Why did this happen? Is this how you treat your servants, your own children?"*

Had this been a burglar, I reasoned, who broke into the house and robbed and killed her, I could have handled that scenario better, since it would have enabled me to fix blame and direct my anger toward the intruder, and not God. But the authorities held God responsible (as I did) for this, and basically charged Him with malice. It didn't make sense. I couldn't explain it, and none of it fit my theology nor did I find anything in my seminary class notes to help.

After all the rationale, all the misgivings, all the confusion, doubts, and fears, I finally settled down. Faith took over and I made a deliberate, willful, conscious decision to trust the character of God—His wisdom, goodness, and ultimately, His love. In the end, I had no other choice. I decided to stop murmuring against God and withdrew my accusations of divine disinterest, misconduct, and worse yet, injustice. I no longer felt the driving need to "defend" God or His actions, neither of which I fully understood. Nor would I make any further attempt to somehow validate and reconcile my faith with shallow explanations and Christian platitudes. Some things are better left for God to unravel and oversee. And that is precisely what I learned outside the seminary campus in God's schoolroom, where people live-out their daily lives facing situations that often defy logic and theological constructs.

Who can explain the carnage of that awful day to the families and friends of those murdered at Columbine High School (1999), Virginia Tech (2007), or Sandy Hook Elementary School (2012), and others more recent? What can be said to a grieving mother, who is struggling with crushing guilt over sending her 12-year old boy on an errand to the local grocery to purchase a loaf of bread, only to learn later that he was struck and killed by a car while riding his bike to the store?

Who can comfort the family and friends of a beautiful, baby boy born with a heart defect and needing immediate open-heart surgery, followed by sixteen, long years of repeated, medical procedures to repair the damage? In the end, his parents stood for fifty-one days at their son's bedside, hoping, praying, believing God for a miracle. They were wonderful people, who had spent their lives serving the Lord. Hundreds from across the world were praying. Throughout the ordeal, the boy's family remained hopeful, holding firm to their faith, trusting God to heal their son; even convinced of it. Yet, he died. Afterward, his mother wrote of the *"rage and anger… regret and guilt"*, and the immense sadness, *"the heartache, the kick in the stomach, the feeling of overwhelming grief is so very real."*

A distraught friend wrote to the parents:

It's all just so incomprehensible. The situation, your pain, God's plan…I can't bring myself to share this with my little girls, who will crumble into tears for the boy they didn't know, but prayed for fervently… <u>I have no answers for them</u>, and frankly, I start to crumble, too, when I think about it… I pray for God to heal the raw, gaping wounds your hearts are experiencing right now. And I pray He will stay close to you and that you will feel His presence during this long dark night.

No words of explanation for the tragedy were offered, just a friend praying, weeping, and standing in the "trenches" with those who were hurting so deeply. The personal touch of a compassionate friend and a simple prayer for God's intervention was effective. It always is. One year later, on her son's birthday, the mother of that sixteen-year-old boy shared the hope of her heart.

> *We may not know the answers to so many questions, but that's ok, we know where you are and… we will always reflect on the wonderful life you had and the wonderful gift you were to us. We miss you so very, very much. We love you very, very much. We can't wait to see you again soon.*

Such healing only comes from the presence of God, who surrounds and penetrates the soul with the truth of the Gospel that there is good news and hope for tomorrow even in the face of tragedy. The heartfelt plea to answer the question, "Why?" is not always about the demand for additional information or explanations. It is the deep cry of the soul for comfort and for the strength to carry on and face the "long dark days" ahead. It is the human spirit needing to *"be still"* (NIV) and *to "cease striving"* (NASB) regardless of external appearances, knowing that there is a God, a God, who is *"a very present help in trouble"* (cf Psalm 46:1–11, NASB). It is a critical lesson for the pastor and every believer. It is *that* or face a crisis of faith.

Mother Teresa, one of the most famous religious figures over the last century, lived much of her life working among India's poor and dying. She won the Nobel Prize for Peace in 1979 for her extraordinary service. In her letters and private reflections, she revealed her own deep, personal struggles as she searched for God in the dirty, diseased, poverty-stricken streets of Calcutta. She did not see Him in the barren and battered lives of the poor. She wrote, *"In my heart, there is no faith. I want God with all the powers of my soul, and yet between us there is terrible separation."*[2]

Frankly, some days I hung by my fingernails on the precipice called the sovereignty and character of God. Experience quickly taught me that in the end there is little else. I learned that sometimes it is better to sit quietly, like Job's three friends who eventually shut their mouths, and offer no words to soothe *"the raw, gaping wounds"* of a broken man or battered woman. There are moments when answers are in short supply—just tears and confusion.

I had the privilege of conducting the funeral of a wonderful young man who had a big smile for everyone he ever met. Kyle was a faithful husband, a loving father, and a decorated war hero. Family and friends loved him, and his peers greatly admired him for the courage and trustworthiness he displayed on the battlefield. He was diagnosed with an aggressive form of cancer and eventually died. For two long, agonizing, hard years, he suffered terribly and fought the disease with every ounce of strength he could muster, but in the end, he lost the fight. Watching her precious son endure so much physical and emotional pain, Kyle's mother asked the obvious question

Why? Why dismantle this fine, young man, piece-by-piece—a soldier, who has survived war, a wonderful husband, the loving father of a beautiful, two-year-old, little girl? Why take him a part? Why destroy his hopes and dreams first and put him through so such misery? For God sake, just take him and be done with it! It would have been easier to have lost him in battle over Afghanistan" (He flew Apache Helicopters for the military)... *I'm really searching for where God is in this.*

All I could do was listen. I could offer no comfort—nothing that would have brought immediate relief and understanding to a mother's broken heart. The seminary classroom was empty of any significant response or suggestions, and I had to accept the fact that in times like these answers are hard to come by.

We often find ourselves at a loss for words. Philip Yancey concluded,

THE DEEP DARKNESS—DOUBTS AND FEARS

There is nothing much you can say to help suffering people. Some of the brightest minds in history have explored every angle of the problem of pain, asking why people hurt, yet still we find ourselves stammering out the same questions, unrelieved.[3]

I can still recall the day we moved into the parsonage of a local church. It was my first pastorate. A little 5-year-old girl came walking down the street, as we were unloading the moving van. She lived but three houses down and had found her way to our home to meet the new little girl (our daughter) who would soon become her playmate for the next fourteen years. They became the best of friends and spent hours together playing dolls, giggling, and just having fun. Gail grew up in our home and became one of the family. Fast forward to post high school. Gail was on the way to her father's class at the local community college where he worked. Her car hydroplaned, and she was killed on impact.

I will never forget that afternoon when the phone call came into my study. Gail's mother called me. I picked up the phone.

"Hello."

"*Pastor, Gail is dead.*" I instantly recognized the voice on the other end. It was my neighbor.

At first, I didn't want to believe what I had just heard. It wouldn't register. So, I asked, "*What?*"

Her mother repeated her statement, "*Gail is dead.*"

I went to the emergency room with the parents to identify the body. And there, before my tear-filled eyes, lay the lifeless shell of a once vibrant, young lady—gone at the age of nineteen. There was shock, sadness, and bewilderment. This didn't just happen, did it? How could this be?

No doubt, that was the hardest funeral I ever conducted. Following the service, family and friends gathered at the parent's home. Later that afternoon, Gail's father was standing at the front door looking out into a dark, gloomy sky. I walked up to him, put my arm around his shoulder, and asked how he was doing. He paused for a moment before responding and then said something that penetrated to the deepest parts of my soul. I will never forget his words. He looked at me with tearful eyes, and said, *"Thank you."*

I asked, *"Thank you for what?"*

He whispered, *"Thank you for not trying to make sense out of this whole thing."* Lesson learned.

Seminary might have informed me about the sovereignty of God and the theology and hope of the resurrection (and there is much comfort in that), but no academic institution or university could teach me the depth of emotion and the incomprehension behind the words of that man and the spiritual assault on his soul, as he struggled with his faith in a place where God seemed absent and His goodness was being called into question. That lesson is only learned in the deep darkness, in the harshest of life's events, when doubts and fears exact their toll on a person's faith. Lectures and PowerPoints just don't seem to get the job done.

Tragedy with no apparent purpose hurts more deeply than one that seems deserved. We understand, demand, and value justice, because it seems right, and we expect to see it played out in our daily lives. However, when injustice invades the sanctity of life, questions abound and often remain unanswered. In fact, the pastorate and ministry in general have left me with more questions than I have answers, answers that a seminary degree alone couldn't possibly have provided.

While I was teaching in Italy, I met a missionary who had been a church planter for many years. He and his wife opened a store-front church in the middle of a bustling city in northern Italy. His wife had become ill and was struggling with a debilitating, progressive disease. Over dinner I asked him how she was doing. He told me that she was bedridden and needed to be propped up with pillows to keep her upright. I could see the pain in his eyes. I probed a bit further and asked how he was managing all this and if he and God were still on talking terms.

THE DEEP DARKNESS—DOUBTS AND FEARS

He opened his Bible. I thought for a minute that in response to my question he was going to read me a Bible verse that had come to personally mean a great deal to he and his wife. For a moment, I thought he was going to "play church," and tell me what he thought I wanted or needed to hear. Instead, he took out a picture of his wife that he carried with him everywhere he went. It was pressed between the pages of his Bible. He sighed, as he showed me the picture. She was younger then and vibrant, so full of life—a beautiful woman who had faithfully stood with her husband throughout his ministry years. They were a team, serving the Kingdom of God. He looked at the picture and mournfully whispered, *"Yes. I still talk to God, but I have a real problem with Him. I am disappointed with Him. I wanted more from Him. I demanded more. I expected more... and nothing. He has just got to do better than this."* Such brutal honesty.

Heartbroken and befuddled, I sat quietly, blinded by my own outrage and fears. I had little to say, feeling a close kinship with *"all the king's horses and all the king's men who couldn't put Humpty-dumpty together again."* There was nothing in my classroom notes that might have helped me or him, though I desperately wanted to do so.

What I could not spiritually grasp in the early years of my ministry was the miracle of God willingly involving Himself in the sorrow and pain of this world. That is the remarkable story of the incarnation and the Cross (more on that later). It is at the heart of the Gospel, and I would see the action and drama of God entering into human suffering and wasted lives over and over again. That lesson starts and finishes with the revelation of Christ's redemptive, sacrificial actions at Calvary, where Jesus suffered terribly and carried the weight of the world's sin on his shoulders, an innocent man dying for the guilty. He willingly hung between heaven and earth. Beaten, broken, and bleeding, He raised His eyes heavenward, and asked, as so many do when hell has broken loose in their lives, *"Why has Thou forsaken me?"* For a few brief moments that must have seemed like an eternity, Heaven was silent. No explanation came from above, just the agonizing, muffled sounds of a dying man struggling to breathe. The question, *"Why? Why this? Why now?"* is the deepest cry of a broken heart and a wounded spirit.

Eventually, every *"Why?"* must be surrendered to God, who alone knows the end from the beginning and how all things fit together in the divine plan: *"Father, into Thy hands, I commit* (entrust for safekeeping) *My Spirit" (Luke 23:46, NASB).* Sometimes that was all I had, when life got hard for so many. Sometimes that's all there is. Either life and death serve some eternal purpose and greater meaning, or they do not. Either trust God with what I don't understand and cannot intellectually, emotionally, and spiritually unravel or rationalize to my satisfaction, or don't trust Him. There is nothing else—not really, just the mystery of the divine scheme.

The prophet Habakkuk was displeased with life and angry at the unchecked evil of his day. He prayed for relief, but God seemed silent and indifferent toward his predicament. *"How long, O Lord, will I call for help, and thou wilt not hear?"* (Habakkuk 1:2, NASB)—a question every person, including the pastor of a local church, will voice frequently.

God set the record straight and informed Habakkuk of His plan—a plan so farfetched, so inconceivable and extraordinary from a human perspective, that the prophet couldn't believe it—wouldn't believe it, even if the Lord Himself told him, and He did (Habakkuk 1:5). God had the audacity to do the unthinkable—use the Chaldeans, outright pagans, a *"fierce and impetuous people"* (1:6) to bring divine judgment and correct all that had gone wrong. This proved problematic for the prophet, since the actions of God were irreconcilable with Habakkuk's theology, a situation most common among finite creatures (and that includes the seminary graduate), who cannot fathom an infinite God doing the things He said He would do and doing them in a manner that seems inconsistent with one's understanding of who God is and how He works. Like all of us, Habakkuk would have to learn to *"live by his faith"* (2:4). There was no other choice in the face of circumstances he neither understood nor fully comprehended. The prophet finally conceded *(Habakkuk 3:17-19, NLT):*

...even though the flocks die in the fields,
and the cattle barns are empty,
yet I will rejoice in the Lord!
I will be joyful in the God of my salvation!

When I was confronted by tragic events that defied explanation in my own life and in the lives of the people I served, I began to better understand the necessity to *"walk by faith"* and *"rejoice in the Lord,"* though evil may appear to momentarily have gotten the upper hand. Consequently, I learned to stop my fruitless attempts at trying to figure things out. The best education in the world could not and cannot adequately square the harsh realities of life with theological systems and doctrinal beliefs. I would have to find another classroom that was better equipped to help me learn what was needed most in ministry, my ministry—simple trust and hope in God.

Catherine Marshall, known for her inspirational writings, battled tuberculosis for much of her life and suffered the heartache of her husband's sudden death. Her life, by her own admission, was anything but *"easy straightaways."*[4] There were unexpected twists and turns in the road she traveled. However, in those horrifying moments of disruption and uncertainty, she learned some valuable lessons about God, lessons that could only be taught and appreciated in crisis, not in a safe, cozy, academic setting.

She observed,

The word 'impossible' melts away with Him. He knows no defeat; can turn every failure and frustration into unexpected victory... With Him a seemingly dark and desolate future becomes a joyous new life. I know all this to be true because I have lived it. I have met God at moments when the straight road turns... and He has picked me up, wiped away my tears, and set me back on the path of life.[5]

The pastor, ministry leader, and follower of Christ will rarely ever find acceptable answers for unexplained hardships and unexpected trials, which includes the bitter disappointments and disillusionment that often accompany such painful events. Much of life will remain a mystery. Pre-packaged, theological sounding, pat answers do not work or play well on the street. Something more is needed—experience, experience with God in those dark and desolate places. The answers come only from having "lived it."

Three months out from Egypt, Israel found itself in the wilderness where God summoned Moses to the top of Mt. Sinai to give him a list of life's most important and basic commandments, ten of them to be exact, designed to govern and guide the mundane affairs of everyday life. While waiting at the base of the mountain for Moses to return, the people saw what appeared to be the *"smoke of a furnace."* They felt the mountain quake with violence beneath their feet; watched as lightning flashed across the sky, and their hearts melted in fear with every crack of thunder. The sound was deafening, and the people were understandably terrified.

The following words were recorded and preserved in the annals of biblical history, *"As the people stood in the distance, Moses entered into the deep darkness where God was"* (Exodus 20:21, NLT).

The last phrase of that verse truly intrigues me—the place where God was/is to be found—in the *"deep darkness."* That gives hope for the pastor and ministry leader trying to comfort people who are *"terrified"* by the perplexing and hurtful circumstances they are facing. I must admit that even after years of experience in ministry and a solid seminary education behind me, I remain to this day woefully inadequate to walk with people through their theological and individual valleys of darkness.

It seems that God is not often found under the bright lights of personal success, nor during trouble-free days. He is not necessarily in the joys and pride of great achievements, awards, and human promotions. He is certainly not in the applause of the crowd.

THE DEEP DARKNESS—DOUBTS AND FEARS

To the contrary, God seems to show up when I find myself wandering through my own desert of sorts without direction or any real purpose, desperate for a sure word of comfort or challenge. It is in those difficult, trying, chaotic moments of daily life that God presents Himself, connects Himself, reveals Himself to those (pastors, leaders, and disciples) brought low, confused, and unnerved by the unsettling, troublesome direction life often takes.

It doesn't matter what is, or what has been, or what will transpire in the days ahead, because I have learned that in the "deep darkness" God shows up! He always does. Look for Him *there* in *that* place!

WHERE IS GOD?

"Yet when he (Jesus) heard that Lazarus was sick, he stayed where he was two more days… Lazarus is dead" (John 11:6, 14, NIV).

Where is God
   when I need Him;
When life gets
Dangerous,
   Dreadful,
     Diseased?

When
Moments of unexpected,
Unimaginable
   Heartbreak
Intrude
   Invade,
     Impede my daily routine.

Assaulting my faith
Pressing hard against
   the boundaries of sanity and sanctity.

My mind wanders down dark,
Crooked paths.
Wondering if God will step in,
   Waiting for things to get better.
   Wishing things were different.

How often,
   I whine,
"Unfair!"
    "Unjust!"
       Unnecessary!"
When
The thing feared most comes upon me.
   "Where is God?"
The heart weeps,
   "Lord, if only You were here…"
The desperate,
   mournful words of two hurting souls,
Mary and Martha,
   Who thought…
God <u>*could*</u> have done something,
    <u>*should*</u> have done something.

Mercifully,
   Jesus shows up at tombs.
He <u>***likes***</u> doing that.

Count on it.
   In hospital rooms,
      The marketplace,
         The unemployment lines.
            The divorce courts.

No!
I am not alone… ever!
I am not forgotten.
   The Resurrection and the Life. (John 11:25)
Rises,
   Redeems,
      Rescues.
The God who has never run from pain,
   especially mine,
      is near;
   In the pits of despair
   In loneliness and isolation,
   In the courts of false accusations and rejection.
In a battle with fierce giants,
Courage comes to win the day.

FINALLY,
   like the countless saints of old,
I can begin to
   recline,
      relax,
         rejoice,
"For the Lord is near." (Philippians 4:5)
The truth declared.

"He is risen!" (Matt 28:6)
And once again,
    the heavens trumpet God's promise
    across the universe.
"I am with you always,
    even to the end of the age." (Matthew 28:20)
To STAND BY YOU,
    STAND WITH YOU
        STAND UP FOR YOU.

Where is God?
    The answer is certain.
In troubled waters,
In the furnace,
In the arena where a man's faith is severely tested.
Where is God?
He is near!
    He is **HERE**!
Now and forever.
Let **PEACE** reign supreme.

~ Sandy

*"Because your heart is lifted up
And you have said, 'I am a god,
I sit in the seat of gods
In the heart of the seas';
Yet you are a man and not God,
Although you make your heart like the heart of God"* (Ezek. 28:2, NASB).

CHAPTER 3
THE HEART OF THE MATTER—SIN

In the early years of my pastoral ministry, a woman came to see me for counseling. She entered my office and took a seat opposite me. After the usual greetings, I asked her why she wasn't talking to her own pastor, who recommended me to her. Without hesitation, she responded, *"Well, he doesn't listen very well."* The warning lights went off on my "dashboard." It wasn't long before I discovered what she really meant, *"He doesn't tell me what I want to hear."*

I asked her what was going on in her life that brought her to my office. She said, *"I am afraid."* I asked, *"Afraid of what?"* She immediately opened her pocket book and pulled out three standard size pieces of paper. She began to read a list of fears. Among her numerous phobias, she said she was afraid of her children—that they didn't love her; afraid of her boyfriend; afraid of getting up in the morning to face the day; afraid of what *might* happen. She was afraid of being alone. I just listened with little or no comment other than an occasional question for clarification purposes. Nothing was settled.

Two days later she returned to my office and picked up right where she left off. She continued.

"I'm afraid of the future... I'm afraid of death and dying. I fear the dark... I fear the Devil and demons... and angels, and I'm afraid of God. I'm afraid of going to hell and not going to heaven, when I die."

I asked her to give me a little background regarding her life, including her past and present decisions and behavior, since life does not happen in a vacuum. I was hoping this information might help me to better understand why such fear had dominated her thinking and overwhelmed her spirit, though I already had my suspicions.

She married at sixteen, because she was pregnant with twins. She divorced her husband six months later. I asked her why the divorce? She calmly said, *"He didn't turn me on anymore."* Her response was disconcerting and alarming. She indicated that over the next five years there were numerous men coming and going in her life. She seemed quite pleased with herself, though no relationships were ever found to be fully satisfying. She then told me that she had recently returned from Florida with her current boyfriend.

She bragged (and that is not an exaggeration) that the two of them had gotten so *"stoned"* during their trip that the next-door neighbors had to come in and take care of her twin girls for three days. The couple had no idea of where they were or what they were doing. They had lost touch with reality.

At this point, I could feel the anger rise-up within. I'd had enough. I interrupted her, looked her straight in the eye, and forcefully said

Now, let me get this straight. You're telling me that you went down to Florida and shacked-up with some guy for three weeks, knowing full well that God wouldn't want you to do that, but you went ahead and did it anyway, and then got so high on booze and drugs that you couldn't take care of your own kids and you put them at risk—no longer able, as their mother, to insure their safety and well-being? I'll tell you what, honey! If I had your track record and did half the things you did, I'd be scared to hell of God, too!

I went further.

> *What you need is plain old-fashion repentance—change your thinking and change your behavior. Start doing what God wants you to do and you can get rid of these fears. You don't have to leave this office the same person as you came in. You can walk-out of here free from all this. Things can change. You can change.*

No sooner did I get the word *"repentance"* out of my mouth, the woman got up, put her coat on, and walked out the door. Nothing did in fact change. There was no evidence of genuine regret or sorrow—a *"sorrow"* that leads to *"salvation"* (II Cor. 7:10, NASB).

The heart of the matter was/is sin. It is everywhere, even in the life of a young mother with twin girls. Sin is the world's real problem—a reality I never entirely grasped during my academic training. I simply didn't get it. I didn't realize, nor fully appreciated, just how far and wide the depravity of man had gone, penetrating every aspect of creation and the church I was about to pastor. I could certainly quote the appropriate Bible verses following formal pastoral training and had a basic, intellectual idea regarding the concept of sin, but lacked any significant, applicable, real-life experience and exposure to its catastrophic effects beyond my own life. Like so many I had an optimistic start to my ministry, which formal education and youthful idealism helped to provide. Experience, however, taught me the complexity of the human condition and the prevalence of wickedness. Had I grasped that sooner, I may have felt better prepared.

After forty years in both government service and academia, which included the completion of a seminary degree, a short tenure as a faculty member at a Christian college, and training as a hospital chaplain, a *"co-worker"* (I Thess. 3:2) in ministry, came to a brutal conclusion.

Truly, people are wretched. I have lost all hope that leaders/executives/ politicians, or priests/pastors/ministers, or counselors/psychologists, or social workers/caseworkers, or teachers/educators can make any more than the smallest dent in the sinfulness that is human nature. People are dishonest, competitive, violent, betraying, untrustworthy, self-promoting, selfish, deceptive, greedy, duplicitous, condescending, ignorant, illogical, vindictive, mean-spirited. Christ cannot come soon enough.

The depths of human corruption go deep, and the character of humankind is marred with all manner of cruelty. The human heart (the seat of reason) is exceedingly deceptive and *"desperately sick"* (Jere. 17:9, NAS); ruthlessly and cleverly able to argue for and justify every hateful, self-serving decision and hurtful pattern of behavior. It is *"incurable"* (actually, *"beyond cure"*—NIV), which is what the Hebrew word (anash), used by the prophet Jeremiah, strongly suggests. Sin is inescapable and destructive! It has breached the walls of humanity and invaded the secret places of our soul. Worse yet, *"there is no fear of God to restrain"* all who fall under its influence (Romans 3:18, *The Book*). Make no mistake. That indictment stands constant down through the ages.

There is no minimizing sin's destructive nature and its crushing force. It maims, destroys, and kills everything it touches. The *"wages of sin"* is indeed death… and a man/woman can die a thousand times before his or her feet ever hit the grave. I wish I had taken this fact more seriously prior to ministry, because a personal, genuine consciousness of sin would have certainly reinforced the harsh reality—that the church and the world was and still is a mess, piled high with the "bodies" of broken, bruised, and bleeding people. Malcomb Muggeridge observed, *"The depravity of man is at once the most empirically verifiable reality but at the same time the most intellectually resisted fact."* A few years in the pastorate and I wasn't resisting anymore.

I often asked my undergraduate students to define the term "sin," as they understood it and experienced it in their own personal lives. They inevitably provided a list of destructive activities (murder, adultery, stealing, coveting, etc.). Many listed all or part of the Ten Commandments in their definitions, which proved to be a typical response from the "man on the street." I expected more from Bible students, but honestly, I wasn't much better as a seminarian.

I originally understood sin as a conscious, deliberate act of defiance; that is, willfully and gladly choosing to behave in a manner that is outwardly in disharmony with and disobedient to God's word and will. I once thought sin was simply failing to measure up to the standards set by Heaven and ignoring God's clear directives. In fact, I assumed it was all the above, and then some. The phrase *"missing the mark"* and the biblical term *"lawlessness"* were/are the preferred (and safer), less convicting and more common definitions of sin. I readily and rightly recognized "sins," as an external display of gross misconduct, but that didn't go far enough or deep enough. I had identified the fruit but failed to see the root of it all.

What is it about us; what is in us that would drive a person to do the unspeakable: to mercilessly march six million Jews off to the gas chambers; to line up men dressed in orange jump suits on a beach in the Middle East and then proceed to cut their heads off before a watching world, while justifying their horrific actions in the name of God or some warped ideology? What presses us to speak slander about another, to gossip, to covet what somebody else has been given or to look the other way when someone needs assistance? What moves us to exploit young women as sex slaves; to blow up a crowd of bystanders at the Boston Marathon, or in the streets of Paris, or Brussels? What drives a man to fire an automatic weapon from a motel room into a crowd of concert goers in Vegas, killing 59 people and wounding more than 500 others? What is it that provokes an individual to beat and abuse children, to walk out on their spouse? What prompts a citizen to shoot a police officer seated in his squad car, or a police officer to shoot an unarmed citizen? What is it that produces all manner of prejudice and hatred and racism? Christian philosopher, Dallas Willard (onetime professor at the University of Southern California's School of Philosophy in Los

Angeles from 1965 to 2012), was asked if he believed in *"total depravity."* He responded, *"I believe in 'sufficient depravity'. I believe that every human being is sufficiently depraved that when we get to heaven no one will be able to say, 'I merited this.'"*[1] When unmasked, sin is an ugly matter.

Many years ago, the ministerial counsel of which I was a member met to discuss recent race riots in the local high school. We needed a solution. The consequences of racism were readily identifiable, running through the halls of the community's schools. Fists were flying. Anger was raging. Accusations and blame were abundant. The root cause needed to be isolated before a solution could be offered. Was the real problem solely intellectual as several ministers, who should have known better, had suggested (students just didn't *know* how to behave)? Or was it related to economic and/or social disadvantages (some had more than others)? Could we solve this problem with education alone or by simply throwing more money at it? We've tried those and failed miserably. Is that the best we can do? Is that all we've got?

It seemed obvious to me that neither approach has worked or would work. All manner of social programs (some better than others and some vitally needed) in the community have been made available to assist people in need. There have been a variety of accessible educational programs at the local, state, and federal levels designed to provide the training and skills necessary for successful entry into the work force and future job placement. The church also has been in the business of educating students from pre-school to the Christian college campus, only to learn that in the final analysis the intellect has never been the real problem. We have produced some really, smart crooks and terrorists!

Today we've amassed an impressive array of programs for the mentally ill, for divorced persons, and for drug, alcohol, and porn addicts. We have opened centers for the homeless, built more prisons (and more churches), increased law enforcement, and passed additional laws. Yet, the problem remains. In addition, the local church has been on the front lines serving in soup kitchens, drug rehab and counseling centers, community shelters for abused women and children, and rescue missions. We've given away food, clothing, housing, Bibles, cars, and cell phones, and still nothing has worked to eradicate human misery and human failure. Neither social programs or education will alter a man's character. Sin is deep-rooted in the fiber of our being.

Os Guinness has concluded,

Put all the self-help philosophies, techniques and seminars together, bring in all the counselors, psychologists and psychiatrists ever trained, and never in a million years would humanity as it was, and is, ever be of achieving a new humanity… the record of history shows, we have not proved capable of transcending the destructive consequences of our innate egotism and violence.[2]

In my early ministry, I was forced to face the frequent, bitter disappointments of ministry. I stood by helplessly, and often frustrated, observing first-hand the many people who were trying desperately to make it—to live out their daily lives successfully and productively, but regularly falling short of the goal. Marriages collapsed. Suicide invaded the neighborhoods. Depression and discontent were commonplace, and traditional values (honesty, integrity, responsibility, hard work, etc.) seemed hard to find.

One highly respected, community official left his wife and children to move in with another man's spouse. Two families were destroyed and the children on both sides were displaced. One man came home and found his best friend sleeping with his wife. Adultery kills relationships. The son of a church leader was arrested and confined to the state psych ward for paranoia due to heavy drug use, and a future was nearly ruined. A young teenage girl, who was a member of a church youth group, was molested repeatedly by her father and feared for the safety of her two younger sisters. The problems were not primarily a lack of education, or social standing, or economic disadvantage. These were symptoms of a much deeper nature.

The fundamental problem was moral. It was a heart issue. Indeed, it always has been a heart issue, and the very reason the Tin Woodman in *The Wizard of OZ* would rather have had a new heart than a greater intellectual capacity. Even he recognized that *"brains do not make one happy."*

Such is the human condition—sin woven into the very fabric of every person's heart. The root of all malice and malcontent; every misdeed, every offense, every hateful, caustic word spoken, and every vengeful, vicious deed ever committed is sin—that unmistakable, undeniable *spirit of independence*—that relentless longing to live for self; that unyielding desire to live apart from God and to live life on our own terms, not God's or anybody else's; that persistent drive to unseat and supplant God as the rightful Lord of all, especially as King ruling over our personal, daily lives. We want the throne. We want the scepter of authority and control. We want to be the only legitimate sovereign to govern our soul. We demand liberty (actually, license) to think and act as we please, but in so doing, we are chained to our own unbridled, self-serving passions and to what C.S. Lewis referred to as, *"inexcusable corruption."* Lewis concluded, *"I willingly believe the damned are, in one sense, successful rebels to the end; the doors of hell are locked on the inside... They enjoy forever the horrible freedom they have demanded and are therefore self-enslaved."*[3] Accordingly, we are under the thumb of an "old master...sin," and thus proudly live, unconcerned "with doing what is right" (Rom 6:18, 20, The Book).

Aldous Huxley, British novelist and philosopher, summed up the problem:

The philosopher who finds no meaning for this world is not concerned exclusively with the problem of pure metaphysics (the fundamental nature of reality); he also is concerned to prove that there is no valid reason why he personally should not do as he wants to...For myself, the philosophy of meaninglessness was essentially an instrument of liberation sexual and political.[4]

And that is precisely the issue. That is the heart of the matter.

Sin is the innate, distinctive, ingrained tendency within humanity to "thumb our nose in the face of God" and at all authority, for that matter—to demand that things *be* and *go* our way, no matter what God or anyone else says. The verdict is in; all stand guilty of "cosmic treason" before the Tribunal of Heaven.

The problem with Adam and Eve and the rest of humanity is that, in our rush to be *"like God, knowing good and evil"* (Gen 3:5), we have behaved like the "Prince of Tyre" (Ethbaal, the father of Jezebel) who was charged with arrogantly laying claim to the throne of God (Ezekiel 28:2). He demanded to *self-define*. From the outset of man's appearance, it was God who defined (and continues to define) for us what is good and what is evil; what is of worth and what is worthless; what is right and what is wrong…and frankly, we would rather do that for ourselves, and have. We want to call the shots, strike out on our own, set our own standards & values, and live *independent* of God's laws and government. The results are predicable. Reshape reality to one's own liking, and the liberty to do as one pleases has no limits or boundaries. Rebellion is the rule of *the human heart*.

> *It matters not how strait the gate,*
> *How charged with punishments the scroll.*
> *I am the master of my fate.*
> *I am the captain of my soul.*
>   ~ *INVICTUS, William Henley*

Sin was unmasked in the Garden of Eden along with the horrific consequences that followed—the certainty of physical death, personal dysfunction, broken relationships, emotional disconnection, spiritual isolation, disharmony, and later, a jealous, destructive rage resulting in the murder of one's brother. From the very beginning of my church ministry, I saw in the lives of the people I pastored and in my own life that same *spirit of independence* which has plagued and invaded every generation, culture, and social structure since the fall of man.

I was surprised. I shouldn't have been, but I was. Maybe I would have coped better had I understood better. But frankly, nothing could have prepared me for what I was going to see—wrecked lives, lonely empty eyes, destructive rage, and the faces of hopelessness.

This is not the typical, popular psychology approach of "I'm-okay-you're okay," or another "everybody-feel-good, self-help" textbook sold at Barnes & Noble. This is about real people with names and faces and families, and the depth of brokenness and pain I could not have fathomed or predicted. This is raw. This is personal. I saw it. I felt it. I lived it. And it quickly became apparent that there was/is no end to the evil man can devise. The front page of any newspaper will tell that story. Swedish screenwriter and film maker, Ingmar Bergman, looked through the lens of his camera and concluded,

> *"The world is a den of thieves, and night is falling. Evil breaks its chains and runs through the world like a mad dog. The poison affects us all. No one escapes."*[5]

I left seminary wanting things to get better, hoping that things could get better, thinking that things would get better. They didn't, they haven't, and they won't apart from God's redeeming intervention. I was soon overwhelmed by the demands of the ministry and the lack of true healing and wholeness in the lives of so many. I needed a positive, workable response to the pain observed everywhere. Instead, like T.S. Eliot, I found myself sitting disillusioned and often disheartened on *"a heap of broken images,"* broken promises, and broken lives with *"no shelter... (and) no relief"* in sight.[6]

There was an elderly man in the local community who had been hospitalized. He was a wonderful man, the pastor of a small, rural church for many years, faithfully bringing the grace of God to the people entrusted to him. He was nearing the end of his days. He was dying. I visited him with the intention to encourage him, lift his spirit, and bring a small measure of God's comfort to his bedside. In retrospect, he ended up ministering to me. The man was the closest thing to a "walking Bible" I had ever met, and it quickly became apparent in our discussions that he had walked and talked with God quite frequently through the years. He lay in his hospital bed, at peace on the doorstep of Eternity, assured of Heaven, and confident in the Cross. He was going to Heaven. He knew it. I knew it.

"Pastor," I said to him, *"you and I both know that you are going to see Jesus very soon."*

He smiled and nodded his head in agreement. I recognized an opportunity and took full advantage. Frustrated with my own lack-luster experience in the pastorate, I made a simple, honest, but bold request:

"Pastor, when you see Jesus, please remind Him that there is a young preacher down here who needs to hear from Him from time to time; who is struggling; who needs Him to show up every now and then. I need help. I can't do this without Him. Just tell Him that" (as if God didn't already know).

He promised, he would.

In J. R. R. Tolkien's epic, *The Lord of the Rings: The Two Towers*, King Théoden, who had taken refuge in the mountain stronghold at Helm's Deep, was eventually forced to come to terms with his own failure and inability to protect his people from impending danger, a humiliating defeat, and certain death. An army bred by evil for war had breached the thick walls; a strong, vicious, merciless enemy, intent on methodically destroying the lives of men and women, rushed in for the final kill. Helpless and hopeless, the king laments, *"So much death. What can men do against such reckless hate?"* The answer is nothing.

The Gospel remains the only viable answer to a world gone mad, because it *alone* is able by the power of God to transform the human heart dramatically and decisively, and thereby change a man's values, perspective, and behavior. I had finally begun to see more clearly and truly that the world needs a savior, a rescuer, a liberator—and it wasn't me. Christ and the Cross were the only feasible solution to the human dilemma. No wonder Spurgeon cried, *"When I cease to preach salvation by faith in Jesus, put me into a lunatic asylum, for you may be sure that my mind is gone."*[7]

I had terribly miscalculated what sin has done in this world and in my own life. I had failed to account for what sin would continue to do until the Gospel does its transforming work, Christ returns, and God ultimately brings the curtain down at the close of the ages. By the redeeming power of God, a *"new heaven and a new earth"* will eventually emerge from the rubble of human failure. In the meantime, it will not be easy building the Kingdom of God in a fallen world. With brutal honesty D.L. Moody said

> *"When I was converted, I made this mistake: I thought the battle was already mine, the victory already won, the crown already in my grasp. I thought the old things had passed away, that all things had become new, and that my old, corrupt nature, the old life, was gone. But I found, after serving Christ for a few months, that conversion was only like enlisting in the army—that there was a battle on hand."*[8]

No longer shielded by the idealism and safety of the seminary classroom, I looked at the brokenness in my own life and in the lives of the people I was called to serve. I soon came to the same conclusion as Moody. I was in for a fight on all fronts (more on that later).

In 1758, Robert Robinson penned one of the great hymns of the church, *"Come Thou Fount."* The words of that song ring ever so true today.

> *Prone to wander, Lord I feel it*
> *Prone to leave the God I love*
> *Prone to hear you and not heed it*
> *Prone to scorn you in your love.*

The hymn writer knew what he was talking about. He saw something in himself, and I see it in me. He accurately and painfully described the human flaw. At any given moment, a person can, and often does, ignore God's directions and, in the process, risks the health and well-being of his own soul. The opportunity to reject God's divine mercy and perfect love for something of lesser value is overwhelmingly tempting; so is simply walking out on God, only to later find one's self on a dead-end street going nowhere—one stupid move, if you ask me. But I could do it and have done it. *"When I want to do good,"* the Apostle Paul admitted, *"I don't. And when I try not to do wrong, I do it anyway"* (Romans 7:19, The Message). The pervasive nature of sin dominates daily life. Had I learned that lesson early on in my ministry I may have prayed more fervently and frequently, preached with more clarity and conviction, and leaned more fully on the power of God to do what no mere mortal could do—raise the dead and bring wholeness and healing to broken lives.

One day, Hagar the Horrible, with sword and shield in hand, was thinking to himself, *"I guess it's time to assemble the men for a pep talk, which is tough to do when you don't feel very peppy yourself!"* Boldly, he stood before his men; sword raised high, and shouted,

"You must run 24 miles a day. You must climb mountains and swim icy rivers! And you must go without food or water for days at a time! Men, in order to win the coming battle, you must train long and hard! Only then will you win the battle!"

One of his soldiers stepped forward and asked, *"The men want to know what they have to do if we just want to TIE the battle."*[9]

When it comes to sin, a "tie" isn't good enough.

"Human misery is nearly as old as the human race, but equally old is the story of God's grace, that is, God's mercy to the undeserving"[1] ~ Os Guinness

CHAPTER 4

THE REMEDY FOR BROKEN PEOPLE IN A BROKEN WORLD—GRACE

In *The Hiding Place,* Corrie Ten Boom recorded her sister's words as she lay on a stretcher in a Nazi concentration camp at Ravensbruck. She was nearing her own death. Surrounded by sick and dying people and the dark gloom of hopelessness that lingered over the camp and hospital ward, Betsie whispered: *"… must tell people what we have learned here. We must tell them that there is no pit so deep that He is not deeper still. They will listen to us, Corrie, because we have been here."*[2] Academics alone could not teach me the power of those words, uttered amid such human wickedness and despair. I had not yet been *"there."*

Had I a better grasp of the grace and mercy of God prior to the start of serving as a local church pastor, it may have transformed a rather dismal ministry and produced a more generous and more patient man—one less critical and less condemning. What I didn't know, at least experientially, was that the grace of God makes a miraculous difference in the lives of people. Grace speaks *life to a dying man.* Grace brings *joy to a broken heart, peace to an anxious spirit,* and grace produces *hope for a better tomorrow* for every person troubled by yesterday's failures.

One Sunday morning, I was in the process of locking up the church building when a man, wearing a black leather jacket with the "colors" and patches of his motorcycle gang, walked through the front door. He had chains draped over his right shoulder and wore heavy black, leather boots. He was an intimating sight, to say the least. If I'm honest, I was a bit unsettled since I knew the reputation of gang members.

I asked the man timidly, *"May I help you?"*

He said, *"Can I talk with you?"*

We were alone.

I responded, *"Sure. Why don't we take a seat here in one of these pews?"*

We sat down, and he began to tell me about his life's journey and the many reprehensible things he had done that left him morally bankrupt, emotionally empty, and spiritually dead. In short, he had hurt people and hurt them badly. He was ashamed and sick over the lives he had destroyed and was burdened with the weight of guilt. I remember his sad eyes—the eyes of a soul suffering from severe depression and a heavy heart. He wondered aloud if he could ever find forgiveness for his past.

The biker asked me, *"Can you help me?"*

I responded, *"No. I can't help you, but God can."*

I had nothing to offer, but grace, though I soon discovered that grace was enough. I spoke of the Cross and the message of the Gospel to a guilt-ridden man in need of forgiveness. He listened with intent and then bowed his head and humbly asked God to take the mess he had made of his life, forgive him of yesterday's sins, and give him a new start and a new hope for his future. I witnessed what only grace and mercy can do—set a captive free. The man entered the church with tears rolling down his cheeks but went out with a smile and a new-found joy. It was an early lesson learned beyond the seminary lecture halls that furthered my understanding of the power of God's grace to reach down into the deepest pit of human misery and despair and rescue a lost soul.

The incident reminded me of David who wrote of his own pain.

> My guilt overwhelms me—
> it is a burden too heavy to bear.
> My wounds fester and stink
> because of my foolish sins.
> I am bent over and racked with pain.
> All day long I walk around filled with grief.
> A raging fever burns within me,
> and my health is broken.
> I am exhausted and completely crushed.
> My groans come from an anguished heart (Psalm 38:4–8, NLT).

Nearly every letter in the New Testament begins with the words *"Grace and peace from God the Father and Jesus Christ"* or words to that affect. These are much more than standard, ancient greetings. They are powerful announcements and a common reminder of the Gospel. They are statements about the source of salvation and the reality of reconciliation with God that changes the lives of men and women everywhere for the better.

Grace is God speaking to Jonah "a second time" (Jonah 3:1, NASB), though the prophet at first defiantly turned a deaf ear and ran from God's plan (which he didn't like by the way) to offer mercy to the wicked inhabitants of Nineveh. Grace is God stepping back into Peter's life; once a strong, rugged man, who turned spineless and ran for cover when his faith was challenged. But grace stubbornly refused to let him go. God would not permit him to be defined by yesterday's failures, but rather raised him up to stand firm once again, renewed in faith and love for Christ. Peter would go on to shepherd the early church with distinction and bring the Gospel to the streets of the ancient world, accompanied by *"signs and wonders."* It was quite a turnabout.

An adult student of mine wrote an essay about his personal journey. He described in wrenching detail the tragedy of a broken home, as well as the years he squandered running from God, lost in an endless maze of repeated moral failures. He had desperately searched for happiness and contentment without getting the results he so desired. His story, however, did not end there. His life became a testimony to the mercy and love of God that miraculously transformed him. Today he is walking with Christ. He summed up and described his experience with these words. They need little explanation. He wrote, *"I am drowned with grace!"*

Grace is God stopping a hate-filled, mean-spirited, rock throwing Saul of Tarsus on a dusty, Damascus road to change the course of his life—an undeserving man, who once stood violently opposed to the Gospel, but went on to pen two-thirds of the New Testament. God took him to Calvary, and "drowned" him there with grace, enabling a miserable, wretched man to come to terms with his botched past, and then set him off again to *"walk in newness of life"* on a new journey, in a new direction—old things gone; all things new.

Later, Paul would write of the necessity for all believers to *"feel and understand…how long, how wide, how deep, and how high (God's) love really is; and to experience this love* (personally). He reminded his readers that God's love is so big that *we "will never see the end of it or fully know or understand it"* (Ephesians 3:17-19, NLT). I needed to learn to pray, *"Lord, drown me with your grace!"*

A broken John Bunyan captured the power of God's grace with the words, *"Love lifted me."* And so, it does. *"Great sins do draw out great grace; and where guilt is most terrible and fierce, there the mercy of God in Christ, when showed to the soul, appears most high and mighty."*[3] Bunyan's observation is reminiscent of Paul's words to the church at Rome, *"Though sin is shown to be wide and deep… grace is wider and deeper still"* (Rom 5:20, Phillips).

One word may describe grace. It is found in Psalm 106:44. It is a simple, Hebrew conjunction, just a single stroke of the pen, translated, *"Nevertheless,"* or *"So,"* or *"Then… He (God) looked…"* The word comes on the heels of a list of

Israel's grievous offenses and rebellious acts toward God and the people they rubbed shoulders with daily. They *"sinned... committed iniquity... behaved wickedly"* (v. 6). The psalmist further explained that they forgot God, grumbled, did not listen to the voice of the Lord, provoked Heaven, adopted the practices and standards of pagan nations (not an uncommon practice these days), sacrificed their own children, and *"sank down"* into the depths of depravity—a complete moral collapse. In the middle of all that failure and chaos, grace appeared. It always does. *"Nevertheless"* clearly links yesterday's immoral and unethical actions with God's love being poured out today upon the lives of unfaithful, disobedient people. God *"remembered His covenant... and the greatness of His lovingkindness"* (v. 45).

A similar concept is presented in Romans 5:8, where Paul used the Greek conjunction de *("but")* to connect and contrast the human predicament *("helpless...sinners...enemies")* with the sacrificial love of God shown at the Cross of Christ. This is divine grace in action, replacing divine judgment with divine love. Brennan Manning (1934-2013) referred to this as *"vulgar grace,"* and it is just that, vulgar—humanly speaking, not in *"good taste,"* often a bit offensive, and certainly anything but polite. He explained:

> *My life is a witness to vulgar grace—a grace that amazes as it offends. A grace that pays the eager beaver who works all day long the same wage as the grinning drunk who shows up at ten still five. A grace that hikes up the robe and runs breakneck toward the prodigal reeking of sin and wraps him up and decides to throw a party, no ifs, ands, or buts. A grace that raises bloodshot eyes to a dying thief's request—'Please, remember me'—and assures him, 'You bet!'... This vulgar grace is indiscriminate compassion. It works without asking."*[4]

The concept of grace is certainly not easily understood, especially to people who are painfully aware of their own daily shortcomings and moral failures. Paul wondered why *"this grace was given"* to him—a man by his own admission was *"the very least of all the saints"* (Eph. 3:8, NASB). He had a horrible past—*"a blasphemer and a persecutor and a violent aggressor"* (I Tim 1:13, NASB), who approved the murder of an innocent man named Stephen (cf Acts 8:1). A "vulgar" man by any standard, yet Paul was transformed and *"made a minister, according to the gift of God's grace"* (Eph. 3:7, NASB), and commissioned to *"preach to the Gentiles the unfathomable riches of Christ"* (Eph 3:8, NASB)—an unforeseen outcome for a man with a poor track record. For no reason other than the *"good pleasure of God"* (cf Ehp.1:5), the Gospel amazingly trumps a man's sinfulness. Apparently, grace was God's plan from the beginning and will forever remain a divine *"mystery"* (cf Eph. 3:4), hidden in the depths of God's love.

As age and ministerial experience increased, I became more cognizant of the following realities: 1) A painful awareness of my own sin, shortcomings, and moral failings; 2) A deeper appreciation for and a greater dependence upon the mercy of God, which is and continues to be, offered to unworthy men and women like me, and 3) A growing recognition of the methodical and persistent work of God in my own life and in the lives of others. In short, God has permitted me enough personal failures to teach me something about grace, and thereby keep me generous, humble, and patient with people, particularly those who are seemingly disinterested in changing their negative behavior patterns as I would like, or who are just plain slow to modify the direction of their lives within my timeframe and plan. Fortunately, grace is God's love stretched out over the long haul.

During the early years of my pastorate, the church was involved in a community wide evangelistic campaign. Through the efforts of one of my parishioners, I was introduced to a highly, successful businessman, who was married and the father of six children. He walked into my office and tearfully told his story, a story marred by numerous adulterous affairs, drugs, and alcohol. His life was a wreck, and he was depressed, feeling hopelessly entrapped, beyond help, and on the verge of suicide. Guilt and shame had obviously taken its toll. He wept over his past and worried about his future, knowing he desperately needed forgiveness and reconciliation with God, his wife, his family, his friends, and himself. The Cross was his only hope, for there alone can such a man find grace, peace, and new life. The transformation was immediate, but the story does not end there.

The man eventually moved to a new location across the state, where his business thrived, but his personal life was again falling apart due to poor decisions and destructive behavioral patterns. However, God was not through with this man. Grace came a "second time," knocking on his door—and it came several months later.

My wife and I were heading north on the New York State Thruway. We were excited to be on the way to Lake George to celebrate our wedding anniversary. Traveling at sixty plus miles an hour, Sharon casually looked out her side window, and to her surprise, spotted a familiar face in the car next to us. It had been more than a year since we had seen this man. He was on the way home from a business meeting in New York City. We flagged him down and managed to arrange lunch together. I remember him being seated directly across from me, which made him a bit uncomfortable. After some casual conversation, I finally said,

> *Do you have any idea the probability of us meeting like this, of being on this highway, on this particular day, at this precise hour? You cannot possibly calculate it. We are on a divine appointment. God has stopped you and brought us together, so I can deliver a message—that if you do not stop doing what you're doing and living the way you are living, if you don't change and get back to following Christ, you are headed for disaster. And God wants to spare you that pain.*

He was embarrassed and bowed his head in disgrace but changed nothing. He had heard the divine message and failed to heed the warning of what would most certainly come, if he persisted with his errant choices.

Ten years or so had past and the man had gotten another business promotion along the way. He and his family relocated to a major metropolitan area. He had successfully climbed the "corporate ladder," making a big salary, and was enjoying the prestige, lifestyle, and power that comes with position and rank. Not surprisingly, his personal life had significantly deteriorated. The same destructive, life habits had returned and with them the harsh consequences of a life lived poorly. His marriage disintegrated. His business began to decline, and he lost a son to drugs and possible suicide. He was distraught. Remarkably, grace came a "third time."

We managed to meet at a hotel room in a major city. He was utterly lost—physically, emotionally, and spiritually lower than he had ever been before. He had gone too far, so he thought. He believed that God couldn't possibly want anything more to do with him now—not after all that he had done. I told him otherwise—that God wanted him, loved him, and would restore him. He cried, "I don't know how to get back."

I responded, *"You get back in, the way you first came in—the Cross. Get back to the Cross. You will find God there, waiting with arms stretched wide in love to receive you once again to Himself. It's grace. It's always been grace. It will always be grace."*

Today, he is walking with God, thankful for God's persistent love that would not let him go. I marveled as I watched grace unfold in the life of a broken man.

Some years later, as Resurrection Sunday was approaching, this same person wrote the following:

Happy Easter to everyone and remember it's not about the bunny or about the eggs it's not about your bonnet or the Easter parade. It's all about the risen "CHRIST" and what's been done for you and me. My sins are forgiven, my future secured, it began at CALVARY. Three days later HE rose from the dead, conquered evil, and offered it (love and mercy) to me. Salvation is mine. Glory to God, this captive set free… c'mon get the good life. It's totally free. Sunday is Easter. THANK YOU, JESUS, FATHER, and THE

HOLY GHOST. We (family in Christ) love you, we praise you, and thank you for this the GREATEST GIFT of ALL… AGAPE LOVE and that OLD RUGGED CROSS and JESUS who paid the price for me.

Now, THAT'S grace—*"Marvelous grace… that exceeds our sin and our guilt."*

The observation of God's boundless, unending, tenacious love changed my perspective and my ministry. Grace, I soon realized, is learned in the crucible of life experience. It is one thing to read about grace. It is quite another matter to experience it for one's self.

To think or feel that it is impossible for God to save and sanctify anyone is to exhibit what Oswald Chambers referred to as *"an attitude of defiance"* toward God.[5] I am convinced that grace never overlooks an individual no matter how far they've strayed, how bad they've become, or how unworthy they may seem. Jonathan Edwards said, *"The wonders of divine grace are the greatest of all wonders…that shout, which will ring in heaven forever…"*[6]

The biblical concept of grace includes the idea of *"longsuffering"* (makrothumia), meaning *"staying-power,"* sometimes translated *"patient"* (cf Gal. 5:22, NASB). In other words, God delays His judgement, extends mercy, and does not give up easily, and neither do those who exhibit the fruit of the Spirit. I shamefully admit that I had not consistently applied that truth in my early ministry to the lives of the people entrusted to my care. Unlike the Apostle Paul, I was not always confident that *"He who began a good work in you will perfect it until the day of Christ Jesus"* (Phil 1:6, NAS). C.S. Lewis was correct. *"The hardness of God is kinder than the softness of men."*[7]

Some years ago, I attended the NAIA National Men's Basketball Tournament. My son was playing. He was the co-captain and the starting point guard that year, leading his college team to the school's one and only trip to the "Big Dance." He had a marvelous career—a solid defender, smart with the ball, a consistent, unselfish player, and a threat from the outside. The opening game, however, ended with a loss. His career was over. It was his final game. He would not play another. He knew it. His father knew it. It was finished.

I walked into the locker room following the game to find my son. He had not yet arrived. Apparently, he had lingered a bit longer out on the court. I waited. Finally, the door opened and in he walked. Our eyes met, and we came together in the middle of that locker room and embraced. There was silence. Nothing needed to be said. Nothing should have been said. It was a special moment between father and son.

In those few moments, my mind flashed back over the years. I recalled those times when he was a little boy in the driveway, teaching him how to shoot a basketball. I thought of his days in the local community, basketball leagues, when as an 8-year-old, he would emerge from a group of ten players and race down the court with the ball. I remembered him leading his high school team to a state championship, averaging nearly 28 points a game and being named the state tournament MVP in his senior year. I remember the tears rolling down my cheeks, as I stood in the stands applauding the achievements of my son. I thought of the previous four years and the game winning shots, the joy of watching him play college ball with a passion and an uncommon determination to win. But now, it was over.

In retrospect, it wasn't so much what I thought which I found so remarkable. It was rather <u>what I did not think</u> in those few moments of embrace at the end of my son's playing career. I never thought of those times when he dribbled the ball off his foot. I never thought of that time when he sprinted down the court only to make an errant pass and throw the ball away. I never once thought of those moments when he missed a shot or got angry at an official for making a questionable call. I had not *one* thought of my son's past failures, not even for a second. In the end, I thought only of his successes, his victories, his achievements—those moments when he excelled and surpassed the ordinary and simply did well. And I thought…

Lord, is this the way it is going to be with me and You, when I've come to the end of my life; when my years are finished, my days are complete, the whistle has blown, and the 'game' is over?

I wondered...

When our eyes finally meet in Eternity and we stand face to face, will You lovingly embrace me and share with me those few special moments that only a Father and son can experience, remembering only my successes, only my triumphs, and give no thought to my failures, my missteps, or my misguided decisions and actions?

The answer is found in the simple message of the Cross, in the promise of God, "*And their sins and their lawless deeds, I will remember no more*" (Hebrews 10:17, NASB).

> Grace, grace, God's grace,
> Grace that will pardon and cleanse within...
> Grace that is greater than all our (my) sin.

I didn't learn that in a classroom. I learned it in an old, gym locker room, filled with the musty odor of sweaty uniforms, athletic tape, and wet towels.

Grace works! And that is a lesson worth learning.

Therefore, my beloved be steadfast, immoveable, always abounding in the work of the Lord, knowing that your toil is not in vain in the Lord (I Cor. 15:58, NASB).

"Contrary to what might be expected, I look back on experiences that at the time seemed especially desolating and painful with particular satisfaction. Indeed, I can say with complete truthfulness that everything I have learned in my seventy-five years in this world, everything that has truly enhanced and enlightened my existence, has been through affliction and not through happiness, whether pursued or attained."[1]
~ Malcolm Muggeridge

CHAPTER 5
THE TOUGHEST JOB OF ALL—MINISTRY

In 1914, Ernest Shackleton boarded the Endurance with his team of seamen and scientists to begin what may be arguably one of the greatest survival adventures of all time. They were headed out to the unexplored Antarctic continent. They were there two years for what certainly must have seemed like an eternity, trying to survive in the harshest of conditions with limited supplies, little water, and inadequate shelter. Ice eventually crushed their ship, forcing them to abandon their vessel, and set sail in open boats on two dangerous, but necessary trips across the treacherous, Southern Ocean. Subsequently, they were stranded on Elephant Island, and awaited rescue on an inhospitable, barren, bitterly cold piece of land.

Before the start of the exploration, Shackleton placed an advertisement in the London papers to recruit his crew for the brutal and challenging trip. In retrospect, it seems a bit prophetic. It read:

> *Men wanted for Hazardous Journey. Small wages, bitter cold, long months of complete darkness, constant danger, safe return doubtful. Honour and recognition in case of success.*[2]

Maybe that statement should be included in every seminary and church recruiting brochure.

The ministry, in whatever form and venue in which it takes place (but especially within the local church), is a "hazardous journey," filled with risks and perils at every turn. There is nothing safe about ministry. John Newton (1725-1807) said that *"The Christian ministry is the worst of all trades, but the best of all professions."*[3]

In the final film of the **"Rocky"** series, the aging fighter was pressured to come out of retirement and step back into the ring against an opponent half his age, a man who is faster, stronger, and highly motivated to win. If Rocky agreed to the fight, he would risk being humiliated and disgraced, if not seriously injured. Many rightly thought that the 60-year-old, 2-time, former, heavyweight champion of the world had no chance. Standing outside a neighborhood restaurant, Rocky's son begged his father, *"Do not go through with this. This is gonna end up bad for you, and it's gonna end up bad for me."*

I had a similar response from well-meaning individuals when they heard that God had called me to the pastoral ministry. *"Do not go through with this,"* they warned. They were not happy about my life's direction nor did they encourage me to proceed with the plan. I think they may have known what was coming.

Rocky's response to his son's plea is insightful and applicable:

> *The world* (church ministry) *ain't all sunshine and rainbows. It's a very mean and nasty place, and I don't care how tough you are, it will beat you to your knees and keep you there if you let it. You, me, or nobody, is gonna hit as hard as life* (or ministry)*. But it ain't about how hard you hit. It's about how hard you can get hit and keep moving forward—how much you*

can take and keep moving forward. That's how winning is done (That's how successful ministry is done)! *You gotta be willing to take the hits…* (Rocky Balboa, Metro-Goldwyn-Mayer, 2006)

I'm not sure if theological books and classroom lectures alone could have given me that perspective. The knowledge that I was potentially going to be spiritually and emotionally beaten to my knees as the pastor and/or ministry leader of a local church was a rather disconcerting prospect. Come to think of it, being on one's knees talking things over with God is not such a bad position to be in, especially as the harsh blows land and you must decide whether you are willing to take the hit and *"keep moving forward."* I wish someone would have told me that I was going to get hit and hit hard. I may have learned to duck.

Ministry may be defined as the care and spiritual guidance of people, living out their daily lives in the context of family, community, and church. Ministry is about service and sacrifice, making servanthood its very core. It is the physical and personal extension of God's love, grace, and mercy, employed by men and women called to foster and encourage people to experience success in every area and facet of life. The focus of ministry remains sharp and clear and is designed to help others be reconciled to God, to deepen their relationship with Him, to develop an authentic mature faith that works, to find peace and joy amid a troubled world, and to secure a genuine hope for tomorrow. By any standard, that is a tall order, and certainly not without significant vulnerability, personal sacrifice, and risk to every servant of God.

Nearing the end of my first year as an administrator in Christian higher education, which was preceded by fourteen years in the pastorate, I was forced to replace several staff members for work performance issues. A colleague was concerned for my well-being and sensed the pressure I was under in making such difficult decisions. So, he asked me, *"How are you doing?"* I quickly responded, *"Are you kidding? After being in a church business meeting this is a piece of cake!"* I was quite serious in my response. There is nothing quite like the pastoral ministry.

Just prior to his death, during his 2nd imprisonment in Rome in the spring of 68 AD, the Apostle Paul wrote his last letter to his *"beloved"* Timothy. His letters were both instructive and informative regarding the ministry and they included a stern warning about the challenging days his protégé would face in service to the Lord. It was also a reminder that Timothy's success and survival in kingdom work would heavily depend on God's faithfulness and the supernatural empowering of those intending to serve the cause of Christ. Paul pulled no punches. He clearly laid out the prospects for ministry.

He commanded Timothy to *"join with me in suffering* (not a big fan of that) *for the gospel"* (II Tim. 1:8, NASB) and to *"suffer hardship... as a good soldier of Christ Jesus"* (2:3), to compete *"as an athlete"* with intent to win (2:5), and to work hard like a *"farmer"* (2:6). He wrote to Timothy of *"imprisonment"* and *"chains"* (2:9) (not terribly fond of that either). Paul warned his young apprentice that *"difficult times will come"* (3:1). Some people would be *"unloving and irreconcilable, malicious gossips,"* as well as *"brutal,"* and *"treacherous,"* opposing *"the truth"* (3:1-8) and rejecting *"sound doctrine"* (4:3). Quite the church crowd!

Paul Tripp, writing for *The Christian Post*, stated

> *"The pastoral ministry is war... a deeply personal war. It is fought on the ground of the pastor's heart. It is a war of values, allegiances, and motivations. It is about subtle desires and foundational dreams. This war is the greatest threat to every pastor."*[4]

I recall a bumper sticker pasted on the back of a car that had stopped just in front of me. It was a prayer that every clergyperson or ministry leader who has ever served the local church or elsewhere, for that matter, may have uttered at some point in his or her tenure: *"Dear God, please save me from your followers."* No doubt, the church would be a lot easier to pastor if it didn't have any people in it! Ministry is tough business. Spurgeon strongly suggested, *"If you can do anything else (other than the pastoral ministry) do it. If you can stay out of the ministry, stay out of the ministry."* [5] It is not for the fainthearted. It is demanding, a near impossible task, difficult, and at times, downright painful. It hurts and often cuts deeply into the heart of any man or woman engaged in divine service. Thus, Paul reminded Timothy that the word of God and His presence in directing, transforming, and empowering His servant (II Tim. 1:7, 12; 2:9; 4:17, 19) are absolute necessities. They are non-negotiables in ministry. Timothy would need God's approval and equipping for the work he was about to do, and he must *"kindle afresh the gift of God"* (the anointing of the Spirit for ministry) within him (1:6). Any man or woman who would dare attempt any sort of ministry work apart from the power and presence of God is bound to fail. Be forewarned.

A.B. Simpson, the founding father of the Christian & Missionary Alliance, went further. He declared

> *For any man to presume to represent the Son of God, to stand between the living and the dead, to act as ambassador for Christ, to bear salvation to dying men, to bring men from darkness to light and from the power of Satan unto God, without the anointing of the Holy Ghost, is the most daring presumption and the most offensive impertinence to the God whom he misrepresents and to the men on whom he imposes.*[6]

Ministry is not simply difficult to do, it is IMPOSSIBLE to do without God, and even then, it may (no, it probably will) cost the pastor and ministry leader dearly and personally. Apparently, I missed that class in seminary.

Philip Wagner identified the six major struggles pastors and servant-leaders face in the ministry: 1) criticism, 2) rejection, 3) betrayal, 4) loneliness, 5) weariness, and 6) frustrations and disappointments.[7]

Two other issues of importance surface in the ministry that are commonplace and routine for nearly every pastor I've ever met. They are discouragement and bitterness.

Discouragement

Discouragement is the "heart" being cut from the chest of a servant and left to bleed out on the altar of ministry until every drop of energy and desire to serve is gone. When ministry expectations run high and significant effort is put forth without seeing tangible evidence of personal, relational, spiritual, and/or congregational growth, discouragement becomes routine and gives rise to feelings of failure, self-condemnation, negative attitudes, and a sense of inadequacy. I often thought that I had failed God, failed others, and failed myself when things were not going well or according to plan. One ministry leader confessed to me, *"I fail more often than I succeed,"* a very common, but ruthlessly brutal experience. At times, I felt much like Charlie Brown, who mused, *"Sometimes I lie awake at night, and I ask, 'Where have I gone wrong?' Then a voice says to me, 'This is going to take more than one night.'"*[8]

Spurgeon himself suffered from what he described as *"deep depression,"* and he wrote to his students,

> *As it is recorded, that David, in the heat of battle, waxed faint, so may it be written of all servants of the Lord. Fits of depression come over most of us. Usually cheerful as we may be, we must at intervals be cast down. The strong are not always vigorous, the wise not always ready, the brave not always courageous, and the joyous not always happy... I thought it might be consolatory to some of my brethren if I gave my thoughts thereon, that younger men might not fancy that some strange thing had happened to them when they became for a season possessed by melancholy; and that sadder men might know that one upon whom the sun has shone right joyously did not always walk in the light.*[9]

Several years into the pastorate, I was feeling overwhelmed by the tasks before me and questioned my call to the ministry and particularly my ability to teach and preach effectively. I was convinced that *"The greatest testimony to the grace and power of God was the fact that the church had survived my preaching!"* I quickly became disgruntled and dissatisfied with my performance since the results of my early efforts in the pulpit were negligible at best. I wanted better than what I was producing and set out determined to correct the perceived deficiencies. So, I began to listen carefully to several popular preachers at the time to learn their pulpit mannerism and copy their preaching styles. I believed that maybe, if I preached better, prayed more, and/or counseled differently, things would improve, and I would see more positive results. Not surprisingly, I was unsuccessful and miserable in my attempts to become someone other than myself. I was ready to call it quits.

Shortly thereafter, I attended a Moody Bible Institute pastor's conference. I went with a wounded heart, a dejected spirit, and in great need of renewal. I recall Dr. Stephen Olford (one of finest expository preachers I have ever heard) coming to the pulpit to address more than 2,000 pastors. He looked out over that great gathering and said, *"God does not make duplicates. He only makes originals."* Those few words challenged my thinking and changed my perspective, and ultimately, my ministry. I realized that I only needed to be the man God wanted and equipped me to be—no less than that, but no more than that. I felt relieved and left the conference renewed and strengthened.

Bitterness

Bitterness is another one of those troublesome issues that *"springs up"* (cf Hebrews 12:15) during ministry and church life and will do great harm to the pastor and the people he or she serves. Bitterness is the result of an unforgiving spirit toward those who have treated the ministry leader (and his family) poorly. Resentment and anger readily builds over being harshly and unduly criticized, devalued, and unappreciated for the work and the personal sacrifices made.

I recall one church member who strongly complained at a church business meeting that the Board of Trustees should not give me a car allowance for ministry related travel expenses because *"he (I) would not have to report it as income on his daughter's FAFSA"* (the government's application form for college financial aid eligibility). I later learned that this person's daughter had recently applied for federal assistance and was rightly turned down because the family household income was quite high and thus failed to meet federal guidelines. In comparison, the pastoral salary at the time was quite low and frankly inadequate and so qualified for financial aid. In short, we desperately needed the help if my daughter had any hopes of attending college. I was upset and saw her demand as selfish, spiteful, petty, and terribly insensitive. I felt devalued and the entire incident left me bitter and angry.

Jonathan Edwards, who has been called *"the greatest theologian in American History,"* was charged with being a *tyrant*. Some characterized him as *"stiff, obnoxious,* and *implacable."* Those who knew him were convinced that *"he would not admit anyone into heaven."*[10] Such hostility was meant to malign, to demoralize, and ultimately, to stop the man and his work.

In 1750, after 23 years as the pastor of the Northampton Church, Edwards was dismissed from his duties. He had upset some members of the congregation when he insisted that the Lord's Supper was for Christians only and would not allow the unconverted to participate. Lenient church membership and open communion had been the practice of the church for years, and started by his grandfather, Solomon Stoddard. A dispute developed, and Edwards was out,[11] suffering betrayal at the hands of those closest to him—an all too common experience among those appointed by God to serve.

David endured similar treachery during his reign as king. He was distraught and troubled because those with whom he had *"sweet fellowship together… in the house of God"* (Psalm 55:14, NASB) proved disloyal and violated his trust. He was caught off guard and wanted to run, escape the pain, and *"fly away"* to a *"place of refuge"* (vv. 6, 8). Consequently, he complained to God (v. 17) because he hurt so deeply. Yet, David maintained his hope and *"trust"* (cf vv.22-23) in God to carry him through troubling times. Not much has changed in this regard for pastors and ministry leaders over the years.

Calvin & Hobbs said, *"It's hard to be religious when certain people are never incinerated by bolts of lightning."* I don't remember addressing the issue of strained relationships and conflict resolution to any significant degree in an academic setting! I'm not sure I would have understood it anyway.

Many years ago, an ex-pastor had given some pointed advice to the congregation of a local church. There is pain and anger in his words. The source is unknown, but it is nonetheless brutally honest.

> *If you fear change, both personal and social; if you demand twelfth-century theology and Christianity from your ministers; if you feel that the Christian faith is something to be locked up within the four walls of a church building; if you feel it just and fair to hire a man and his wife—who have together put in approximately 12 to 15 years of study and training for required degrees—to work for you, to be religious for you on a full-time basis for the part-time salary of one unskilled, untrained, and uneducated individual; if you feel that it is a Christian virtue—preparing one for sainthood—to allow one's self and family to be exploited physically, emotionally, spiritually, and financially; then you are probably a typical and average American congregation calling yourself the body of Christ. My recommendation is that you give up the phony church image, put away your pious platitudes, your saccharin sentimentalism of the nineteenth century, blow-out the candles of your churches, lock the doors of your neo-Gothic buildings, and go home and forget the whole thing and become real people.*

No professional training could have possibly prepared me for an experience like that.

In a commentary for *Leadership Journal,* Mark Buchanan wrote of his own pastoral ministry experience.

> *...I didn't know when I first became a pastor that you're a sitting target, a soft wide one. How you speak, what you speak about, your clothing, your smile, your work ethic. That's just the beginning of a very long list of faults. I have been told I'm too loud, too quiet, too theological, too experiential, too driven, too lazy. I bleed. All this cuts me.*[12]

As part of a class assignment, one of my students wrote about the characteristics he thought might be important in searching for a pastor.

> *If I were looking for a pastor, I would look for someone who, first of all, has a strong relationship with Jesus and a passionate love for reaching out to others."*

So far, so good. He continued.

> *I would look for someone with sound reasoning and wisdom through the Holy Spirit to interpret the scriptures, and good communication skills to convey the message to the people. They should know how to speak the truth* (in love, of course) *and how to humbly accept criticism* (that last sentence caught my attention)... (and the pastor) *needs to be favorable to look at.*

That last requirement alone may disqualify many of us!

I responded to the young man:

> *You make some valid points regarding what is important in searching for a pastor. However, some people desire the pastor of a typical, local church to be wearing a pair of blue tights, sporting a red cape, and brandishing a big*

red "S" on his chest, and able to leap tall church steeples in a single bound and fly faster than a speeding bullet to board meetings, community affairs, the hospital, and visitation nights.

Frankly, I'm not sure if Jesus would qualify as an adequate pastoral candidate in many churches. He seems too quick to buck the status quo, turn over the money tables, irritate the religious folk, and challenge the self-righteous.

For a change, it would be nice to hear of the church's responsibility to care for the well-being of its pastors and their families; treat them with respect as those called of God to a most holy task; assist them in the "work of the ministry;" pray for them, and view them as more than a "hired hand" to do for church people what they should be doing for themselves; etc., etc.

Unfortunately, the way some churches treat their pastors is appalling, to say the least, and it fails to honor God <u>before a watching world</u>. No doubt, there are some serving in the pastorate who should not be there; who behave poorly and preach without conviction or passion. But there are many more that are servants at heart and deserve better from the people they selflessly and faithfully serve.

Paul echoed a similar sentiment when he wrote to young Timothy that his *"life has already been poured out as an offering to God"* (II Tim. 4:6, NASB). Honestly, I'm not so keen on the *"poured out"* side of ministry, but it happens, and it should happen. It goes with the job and the call of God upon a man or woman's life.

The Apostle Paul spent himself in the cause of Christ without self-pity or regret. He survived a shipwreck, and later a snakebite, dark prison cells, chains, isolation, misunderstandings, and beatings, all of it with *"special devotion"* to the divine summons. Os Guinness defined the call of God upon our individual and personal lives as *"the truth that God calls us to himself so decisively that everything we are, everything we do, and everything we have is invested with a special devotion and dynamism lived out as a response to his summons and service."*[13]

"Are, do, have, everything" about sums up the life of the servant of God fully sold-out for the sake of ministry. The hymn writer, Isaac Watts, captured the degree of commitment required of all followers of Christ and especially servant-leaders.

> *Were the whole realm of nature mine,*
> *that were a present far too small.*
> *Love so amazing, so divine,*
> *demands my soul, my life, my all.*[14]

No exclusions. No exceptions. No holdouts.

The countless experiences of many a saint through the ages, who answered the call of God to follow Christ in mission and service, stand as a stark reminder of what it takes to minister effectively in this world. There is little doubt that ministry may prove uncomfortable and very costly, but I dare say that the pain *is* necessary. Fr. Richard Rohr agreed.

> *Pain teaches a most counterintuitive thing: we must go down before we even know what up is… Suffering of some sort seems to be the only thing strong enough to both destabilize and reveal our arrogance, our separateness, and our lack of compassion…Suffering is the most effective way whereby humans learn to trust, allow, and give up control to Another Source. I wish there were a different answer, but Jesus reveals on the cross both the path and the price of full transformation into the divine.*[15]

Pain and suffering are transformative for minister and people alike. They are essential, because people in general can sense whether the pastor or the Bible teacher understands and appreciates their personal anguish, that he/she has been *there*, wounded, heartbroken, distraught, afflicted, banged-up, and bleeding. They know whether the man or woman in the pulpit or in the rescue mission distributing food has walked the streets of Hell but has somehow, miraculously, made it out (sometimes crawled out) the other side, having experienced for themselves the staying and healing power of God (cf. II Corinthians 1). *That* pastor, *that* minister, that layperson will be heard because they have become a living testimony that there's hope in Christ, no matter how bad life gets. Credibility opens doors and hearts.

I once believed that if you are going to be effective and redemptive in ministry and have the ability to burrow in under the skin of hurting, suffering people and get down deep into the depths of a wounded soul to pour into their lives the healing balm of God's grace and mercy, *you <u>will be</u> hurt*. I no longer agree with that statement. It is not strong enough nor does it go far enough. I am now convinced that you not only will be hurt, *you <u>must be</u> hurt*. Count on it. Redemptive ministry has always been dependent on *"an Old Rugged Cross, the emblem of suffering and shame"* and the loving, divine sacrifice made by the Son of God on a hill called Golgotha. A servant is not greater that his master.

Frankly, I wanted the *"power of His (Christ's) resurrection"* flowing through my ministry, but I wasn't so excited about sharing in the *"fellowship of His sufferings"* (Phil. 3:10, NASB). I suspect that one does not happen apart from the other.

There is no escape from the reality and role that both trials and tribulations play in the life and ministry of God's servants, toughening and hardening them as they are forged in the sanctifying fires of the Spirit's work, divinely and uniquely preparing each one for the rigors of ministry. Make no mistake. Such divine preparation can be downright painful.

J. Oswald Sanders understood the need. He believed it. He lived it. In his classic *Spiritual Leadership*, Sanders quoted an unknown author who plainly expressed the ruthless and relentless nature of God's work in preparing His servants for effective ministry.

When God wants to drill a man
And thrill a man

And skill a man,
When God wants to mold a man
To play the noblest part;
When He yearns with all His heart
To create so great and bold a man
That all the world shall be amazed,
Watch His methods, watch His ways!
How He hammers him and hurts him,
And with mighty blows converts him
Into trial shapes of clay which
Only God understands;
While his tortured heart is crying
And he lifts beseeching hands!
How He bends but never breaks
When his good He undertakes;
How He uses whom He chooses
And with every purpose fuses him;
By every act induces him
To try His splendor out –
God knows what He's about![16]

In those early days of ministry, I never suspected just *how* acutely I would hurt nor *why* I needed to hurt so deeply. I never quite understood those divine, *"mighty blows"* that most assuredly came to chisel and chip away at the character of a young pastor and ministry leader until he was made useful and suitable for the holy task of ministry, which is the toughest job of all. Lord knows, I needed (and still do need) some hammering.

> *"It is good for me that I was afflicted, that I may learn Your statutes"* (Ps. 119:71, NASB).

"If I get married, I want to be very married." – Audrey Hepburn

CHAPTER 6

THE ALTAR OF STRANGE SACRIFICE—MARRIAGE & FAMILY

Some years back I was invited to preach a weekend series at a church in a major southern city. The pastor was a young man with a wife and two small children. Following the Sunday morning service, we returned to the parsonage for a lovely dinner and what I thought would be a restful afternoon. I couldn't have been more wrong. Before the plates were cleared from the table, the pastor excused himself and set off to do "ministry." His children grabbed onto his pant legs, as he was heading out the door, and sorrowfully pleaded with their father, *"Daddy please don't go! Please!"* Mom pulled them off their father and put her children down for an afternoon nap. When she returned, I was seated in the living room. Her husband had already left on his mission. She sat down and began to cry. I asked her, *"What's wrong? Why the tears? What is going on?"*

She lamented, *"I haven't seen my husband for eighteen days."*

I inquired further, *"What do you mean?"*

She said, *"He leaves around six in the morning and doesn't return home often until mid-night or later."*

"What is he doing?"

She responded, *"He's doing church work."*

"Church work? Seriously? What could he possibly be doing?"

I was hoping to gain a better understanding of the issues, so I might give some measure of guidance and comfort to the young wife of a pastor who was struggling with the toll the ministry was taking on her marriage. I wanted to fix this and offer a possible solution, which most men like doing. Looking for a reasonable explanation to account for the pastor's recurrent absence from his home, I asked, *"Well, how many deacons does he have on the church board that could be called on to assist him in the ministry and lessen some of this burden?"*

She responded, *"Thirty-five."*

I was stunned. *"You mean to tell me that he's got thirty-five deacons and he can't find anyone who might take some of this work off his shoulders?"*

She said, *"No. Actually, he likes doing it himself."*

And therein was some (but not all) of the problem. How insidious the trap. On the way to the airport the next morning, I confronted the pastor. I was brutally forthright and direct.

> *Don't you realize that the very people who are applauding you now for your ministry efforts will be the first ones to go get the rope to hang you, when your wife and children pack-up and walk-out the door of the parsonage? You are a fool.*

I warned him that he would be quickly charged with marital and parental failure, and in the eyes of many (including some denominational administrators), he would be disqualified from further leadership in the local church. In short, he would be forced from his pulpit. As I challenged him, he admitted that he was suffering from depression over this very issue, apparently ignoring his own conscience. I told him I would call him in three months to encourage him and to check on whether he had realigned his priorities and reconnected with his wife and children. I made the call, as promised.

He answered the phone, and after a few pleasantries, I asked, *"So, how are you doing? Have you taken your kids to the playground and spent some time with* them? *Have you gone out on a date or two with your wife since we last talked? Maybe dinner and a movie or even just a walk together?"*

His response was telling. He said, *"I'm doing great. Our baptisms are up. Our budgets are up, and the building project is going well."*

I said, *"That's not what I asked you…"*

I had tried unsuccessfully to convince him that the fleeting, fickle applause of the crowd, even if it is the church crowd, is a poor substitute for a solid, loving relationship with his spouse and children. Not surprisingly, I never heard from him again. Apparently, he didn't want to be *"very married,"* like Audrey Hepburn.

In writing for The Gospel Coalition, author Megan Hill, who was also a pastor's wife, shared her own church experience.

> *More than 10 years ago, on the Sunday when my husband—newly graduated from seminary—was being ordained as a pastor, a godly older man approached us. 'Well,' he said gravely to my husband, 'today is the day you marry this church.' My heart sank. I was ready to be the pastor's wife. But I wasn't ready to be the pastor's other wife.*[1]

One former cleric told me that his wife cried nearly every day for the first few years of their ministry to the local church. They lasted five years and left the pastorate for a secular career. The pressures and strain of ministry can take a heavy toll on a marriage and the home. Another pastor's wife admitted to me, *"I hate the ministry!"*—an unsettling, painful statement to hear from one's spouse. From the outset, the pastor, ministry leader, and layperson must make a conscious and deliberate decision to give his or her marriage and family priority. The pressure to do otherwise is enormous and the consequences of failure are devastating. Outside of an individual's relationship to God nothing is more important to life and ministry than family.

Two years into the pastorate, I was playing a board game one night with my seven-year-old daughter. The phone rang. I excused myself from the table and answered the phone. It was a parishioner, who immediately began to engage me in a ministry-related conversation. I interrupted her and asked, *"Is this an emergency?"* She said, *"No."* I told her that I was busy right at that moment and in the middle of something important. I asked if I might call her in the morning and she agreed.

I hung up the phone and returned to the game. My daughter was still seated at the table waiting patiently for me to get back. I will never forget those big eyes and little pigtails. She looked straight at me and asked, *"Daddy, you did that for me?"*

Little did I know how intently she was listening and watching. The whole phone conversation took no more than a minute. I suddenly realized that I could have preached for a thousand years on how much I loved that little girl and how important she was to me but wouldn't have been more effective in communicating that love than I was in the sixty seconds I had just spent on the phone… and I didn't even know it.

Brian Croft, senior pastor of Auburndale Baptist Church in Louisville, and a senior fellow for the Mathena Center for Church Revitalization at Southern Seminary, observed

> *Marriage is hard enough but add ministry into the mix and you have a recipe for a potential mess… The combined stress of marriage* (and I might add, raising children) *and ministry is a unique situation that demands intentionality to keep both a marriage or a ministry from imploding.*[2]

In retrospect, I wish I had a better understanding of the need to guard my relationship with my wife and fulfill my role as a husband and father. Seminary attempted to address these issues to some degree but was unable to successfully communicate the high level of stress that ministry brings to one's marriage and family. Realistically, the full weight of the problem can only be experienced and appreciated after the pastor arrives at the local church. It wasn't long after we

THE ALTAR OF STRANGE SACRIFICE—MARRIAGE & FAMILY

unpacked that I realized that if I ever hoped to have a quiet, intimate dinner with my wife, we would have to travel to another community on "date night" to avoid intruding but well-meaning church members. In a small town, it was the only way we could get away *"far from the madding crowd's ignoble strife,"*[3] protect our privacy, and insure much needed personal time together.

The potential negative effects of ministry on one's marriage and family are very real and remain a constant source of tension in the home. Awareness of the problem is critical and may serve as the first line of defense. For example, amid the demands of seminary study and the practical side of ministry required of all seminary students, I got a stark and stern warning about the dangers and temptations that awaited those who would pastor the local church or be engaged in other forms of service. The lessons I learned outside the traditional, classroom were painful, but invaluable, and served me well in later years.

While in seminary I got so busy preparing academically for ministry and doing what I perceived to be God's work in the local church (the practical aspect of my education, which I truly loved doing), I failed miserably as a husband and father. Frankly, my priorities were skewed at the time. I fell victim to the *tyranny of ministry* and remained in danger of destroying my own marriage in pursuit of "success." Let every servant-leader beware.

Our family schedules never coincided. Weekdays were taken up with both the demands of a heavy academic load and my wife's evening work hours. She worked hard to keep me in school. She literally would wait each evening with her coat on at the back door of our house for me to return home from the day's classes, so she could make her way to work at a local fabric store. We kissed hello and good-bye in one quick move. Most nights I had dinner alone, put my young daughter to bed, and then settled in for some much-needed study time until my wife returned home from work later that evening at 11 PM. By then, we were both exhausted, drained of the energy and resolve needed for developing and maintaining a healthy, vibrant relationship. It was a breathless, challenging routine. And the weekends were not much better.

My wife worked every Saturday and Sunday, while my weekend ministry schedule was filled with church related activities and responsibilities. Consequently, we grew apart on all fronts and it nearly cost me my marriage and my current and future ministry.

Like the prodigal son, I finally came to my *"senses."* Having realized the magnitude of the problem and the subsequent trouble we were facing as a couple, I said to my wife, *"If you're as interested as I am in saving this marriage, we have got to make a change and make it now, even if it means we pack up everything, leave here, and I don't finish my degree."* It may have been the smartest thing I've ever done or said to her. At the time, I was just one semester from completing my seminary education, but it didn't matter. Nothing mattered but salvaging and restoring our relationship and marriage. We made the necessary changes, and in the end, it saved our marriage and our upcoming ministry (and yes, I did manage to finish seminary). To this day, I remain biblically and experientially convinced that God never intended for a man or woman to sacrifice his or her family on the altar called "ministry."

The tension between marriage and ministry is a common theme among pastors. One attendee at a pastor's retreat confessed,

> *I didn't realize the strain that ministry was putting on our marriage. I knew that it wasn't what I wanted or what it should be. Yet at the same time, I'd just keep going. Then, when we got away for a while, it all came crashing down. I feel like the toll on my family—the damage to me, my wife, and my son—has not been worth the fruit of the ministry.*[4]

Unfortunately, churches often view their pastors as hirelings, an employee of the church, a paid professional, who is employed by the local assembly to fulfill any number of roles and perform an astonishing amount of jobs for its members. In addition to the usual ministry tasks, the weekly duties of the pastor, particularly of a small local church, might include cutting the church lawn, printing the church bulletin, or filling the baptismal pool. I have experienced or witnessed all three and more. The pastor is expected to serve 24/7 (including vacations), all week, all year, everywhere, doing everything, for everybody, and never truly feeling like he or she is off the clock and free from his or her ministry tasks.[5]

A fictitious job posting for pastors puts the problem in perspective.

> *WANTED: Person to teach, preach, and disciple others by offering amazing insights every week. Master's degree required, doctorate preferred. Will actually spend majority of time managing a business operated by volunteers, setting up systems, managing conflicts and politics of competing priorities, and creating and defending budgets. Volunteers will simultaneously be friends, congregants, counseling clients, critics, and the bosses who decide your career path and compensation. You'll work on the day others are renewed and be expected to work the other days 'normal' people are in the office.*[6]

Frankly, who wants that job?

Church search committees often provide a mammoth list of duties, responsibilities, and expectations for their senior pastoral candidates. One such job description I read concluded with this statement:

> *The position requires great flexibility in time schedule* (an understatement, if I ever read one). *The pastor should be available for evening activities as well as work on the weekends. The pastor is free to take one to two days off each week depending on the needs of the congregation.*

And I thought, *"Not a chance of that happening!"*

The toll on the pastor and his family regarding time spent on the job and the daily, energy demands of ministry are extraordinary and rarely appreciated by the average parishioner. Professional and theological training primarily focused on acquiring biblical knowledge and developing the necessary administrative and communicative skills for ministry, but it could not and did not prepare me for the assault on my family's health and the accompanying, constant battle to find balance between being a faithful pastor and a caring, responsible spouse and parent. Research has identified marriage and family as one of five key areas pastors must defend and preserve.[7]

Joe McKeever (writing for *Charisma News*) invited Facebook friends to suggest reasons why someone *"might not want to marry a preacher."* The responses from ministry wives were overwhelming negative. Some said,

- *"The preacher is never at home."*
- *"You are the last of his priorities. Everyone comes before you and the kids."*
- *"The church boards are cruel and selfish and demanding."*
- *"A pastor's wife is never allowed to have friends. I'm so lonely."*
- *"I have wished a thousand times I'd never married a preacher."*
- *"The pay is insulting, the benefits imaginary, and the support from the churches undependable."*[8]

Sometime prior to his resignation over allegations of sexual misconduct,[9] Bill Hybels, the founding, senior pastor of Willow Creek Community Church, received a letter from a church leader who had lost both his ministry and his marriage due to the pressures of the pastorate. It is a letter that challenges every pastor, ministry leader, and follower of Christ about the need *"to slow down."* The man wrote:

> *With all of this, I found myself missing (or conveniently overlooking or justifying) growing signs of problems in my home. Cries for help from my family were drowned out by the roar of the demands of fulfilling my holy calling. When the cries ceased, I assumed the problem had been solved, but it was only that a death had occurred in my relationship with my wife. She now preferred a fantasy relationship with an imaginary lover over the real*

one she had with me. When I found out there was another man in her life, I was crushed. When the divorce came, I was shattered.

For seven long years I never preached or taught. The voice that had ministered to thousands was silenced. The ministry that had won hundreds to Christ, by his grace, was terminated... In my zeal to serve the Lord and effectively use the gifts that he gave me, everything else was viewed as competition and at cross-purposes with the goal I was consumed by. Please, I plead with you, don't let this happen to you. Spend time away from the demands of leadership. When someone points the finger of stinging criticism at you for being away from leadership, think of me. Determine you will not let your ministry and your dreams come crashing down around you like mine did around me.[10]

Experience speaks volumes.

I vividly recall that first morning in my study, as I started my pastoral ministry. God and I got down to business. I was fully aware of my desire and tendency to want to push hard toward succeeding at the task God had called me to do. I was driven to be used of God to bring life to a dying congregation. I was determined not to fail God or His church.

However, God reminded me in those few quiet moments alone with Him of my own past. I knew what it was like to grow up without a caring, attentive father in the home. My father was absent in every respect, and I didn't want that painful experience for my children nor for their mother. So, I made a deliberate, conscious decision—a covenant with God not to neglect my family in the process of pursuing a successful ministry in the local church. The tension was real. Hybels concluded, *"I want to be a faithful pastor, but I want to be a fantastic father; not a mediocre father, and not an absent father. I want to be a fantastic father."*[11] So, did I.

I promised God and myself never to get so busy with ministry that my children and wife would see Him and the church as their chief competitor for what was rightly theirs by divine decree, the love and attention of their father and husband. In the quietness of my study, I prayed, *"Lord, should my children grow and reject the faith of their father it will not be because of my inattentiveness and carelessness."* I would be their pastor, first. I would support them and love them through the best and worst of times. I would teach my kids how to tie their shoes, ride a bike, and shoot a basketball. I would be there to celebrate their birthdays, their academic successes, and athletic achievements, and to pick them up and dust them off when they fell. I would make it my mission to laugh with them and cry with them (and we did plenty of both), and to help them become well-adjusted, productive adults who might grow to love God and love His people.

That focus remained a high priority throughout my ministry and I fought to protect that sacred duty. It was often the little things that made the biggest difference. For example, I shut the phone off every night for one hour during dinner. That was to be our time together to reconnect as a family after a busy day. Nothing except a legitimate emergency was ever permitted to interfere with those sacred moments. Each week I wrapped up study and sermon preparation by Saturday noon to devote the remainder of the day to family, fun activities. I was committed to eliminating distractions and interruptions. Consequently, I informed church leaders and officers not to expect me at a business or planning meeting on nights when there were conflicting family birthdays to celebrate, school activities involving my children, or a wedding anniversary to celebrate. I would not be at the church, and I expected the same from them. I simply learned to firmly say "yes" to that which was important and "no" to that which was of lesser value.

Some years ago, I posted the following on Facebook. It was a critical lesson, learned after many years of life and ministry experience.

> Looking back at the many mountains and valleys of daily life over the years—the good times and the not so good times; the fun times and the hard times; the fleeting joy of a few successes and the crushing weight of numerous personal and moral failures, I've discovered I've got more

questions than answers. However, there is one thing I have come to know for certain:

"You can leave your children and grandchildren all the glitter, glamour, and glory of the world; all the rich treasures of a king; build them bigger barns to store their wealth, and in the end, you have left them nothing of any lasting worth. If, on another hand, you have left your children Jesus, and little of anything else, you have left them everything—everything they will need for this life and the life to come."

When all is said and done, and I near my last breath...let these final words resound down through the corridors of eternity; let my life declare this simple, yet profound truth:

"I'd rather have Jesus, than anything… This world affords today."

I believe it more so today than at any other point in my life. Marriage and family should be and must be a priority in the church, and it starts with the pastor leading the way.

Like any man, I will die with my fair share of regrets for the things I've done and failed to do. However, the one regret I will not have at days end, when eternity is just a few steps away, is that I didn't spend enough time with my wife and children (and now my grandchildren). If I've done nothing else, I've accomplished that, and I'm glad I did. Go thou and do likewise.

Beatle Bailey was still in bed sleeping when the sergeant came into the barracks. He screamed, *"Is that you still in bed, Beatle?"* Unsure of himself, Bailey responded, *"I guess it's me."* He then sat up in bed, picked up a hand mirror, looked himself in the face, and concluded, *"Yeah! It's me alright!"*

CHAPTER 7

THE SEARCH FOR AUTHENTICITY—IDENTITY

I married a PK (preacher's kid). Sharon grew up in the shadow of the local church, watching her father Dave dutifully fulfill the role of a pastor. He was a wonderful man with a gentle heart and a deep love for God and God's people. He was faithful and very busy. He religiously prepared his sermons, led the Sunday morning and evening worship services, taught Sunday school, ran the mid-week prayer meeting, met with the youth and church boards, visited the sick, and often drove his old station wagon weekly into the neighborhoods that surrounded the church to pick-up children and take them to Sunday school. He gave himself unselfishly in service to Christ and the church. Sharon watched that man function in ministry. She heard him preach and observed him ministering to the people entrusted to his care.

Dave was also a peacemaker; rarely would he do or say anything that might disrupt the status quo. He was a nice man, quiet and nonconfrontational (unlike me). My wife's expectations of what a pastor should be were deeply entrenched in her thinking. Over time she observed her father and learned what it meant to wear the mantle of a pastor. I should have taken notes.

In my first few years on the field, I was trying to figure out who I was and what sort of pastor I wanted to be. I had no specific image in mind or a reference point from which to draw. Though seminary provided me with an academic foundation for pastoral duties and responsibilities, it could not give me significant hands-on ministry experience that may have helped me to define my identity and the role of a pastor and ministry leader. Consequently, I spent many months "flying by the seat of my pants." I was raw. Before I could ever put on my clergy collar in the morning for ministry with any degree of consistency or certainty or even lace up my Nikes for my daily trip to the gym, I had to find out who I was, define my identity more clearly, and tighten my grip on God's calling if I was ever to "get in the game." I needed some help to confirm my uniqueness as an individual and my calling to the pastoral ministry, and God did just that, as I met Him in His Word and in the "secret place" of a person's heart where the internal call of God is heard.

I remember a special night when I was working with the church youth. A question flashed before my mind while I was standing in the back of a darkened sanctuary where the youth choir (which I had started) was practicing for an upcoming concert. No words were audible, just a powerful and distinctive thought that suddenly and deeply penetrated my soul. *"Wouldn't you like to serve Me the rest of your life?"* I immediately responded, *"Yes!"* It was a job offer I could not resist. In an instant, my identity, as one called of God to kingdom work began to take shape. That moment began the process of defining who I was and giving clarity to my future role, what I was to do both in the church and in the world.

Jesus revealed Himself to Zacchaeus as, *"The Son of Man"* who has *"come to seek and to save that which was lost."* The *"Son of Man"* was His identity. His role was *"to seek and to save"* (cf Luke 19:10, NASB). Likewise, how I viewed myself was critical to the performance of routine pastoral duties. It drove my daily decisions and actions and influenced the way I handled stress and conflicts, the enthusiasm I exhibited for proclaiming God's Word, and the fulfillment of God's overall mission for my life and ministry.

Identity is about integrity, simply being true to who I am (authenticity), true to the man God designed me to be. Identity is the composite of all my distinctive moral qualities, beliefs, and personality traits. It includes my God-given strengths and weaknesses, skills and abilities, likes and dislikes, values and attitudes, hopes, dreams, and aspirations. Most importantly, identity embraces my standing before God "in Christ" and in His kingdom which explicably and descriptively marks, defines, and makes me (and you) a particular and peculiar individual, *"set apart"* for some divine task and purpose in this world (cf Rom 1:1). There is a sense of uniqueness, distinction, and uncommonness in the concept of identity, an objective reality that cannot be denied. In other words, no one else is quite like me in this world. I am not who the church says I am. To the contrary, I am who God says I am (and so are you).

Bruce Gerencser issued this warning to those entering the local church ministry, as well as to those who are already serving in a pastoral or leadership role. *"Don't confuse your self-identity with the church. Far too many pastors allow themselves to be swallowed up by the church, losing their self-identity in the process."*[1] He is right on target.

It took years of personal experience and floundering in ministry before I could come to terms with who I really was, surely a transgressor of God's law (no one could deny that), but one upon whom *"the riches of His grace"* had been freely given (cf Eph. 1:5–9). The law (not formal schooling) drove me to the cross where I plainly and painfully saw my shortcomings and sinfulness against the backdrop of God's love and grace. There at the cross a man's true identity is shaped, and so was mine, once a *"dead"* man, but now *"He gave (me) life... raised (me) from the dead... created (me) anew in Christ Jesus, so (I) can do the good things he planned* for (me) *long ago"* (cf Eph. 2:10 NLT).

The Bible and the chronicles of sacred history are filled with similar stories of people from every walk of life (princes, fig pickers, fishermen, doctors, etc.) who

THE SEARCH FOR AUTHENTICITY—IDENTITY

took hold of their identity and then spent their remaining days doing and being the men and women God had designed them to be. Moses was such a person.

After he spent forty years tending sheep in the deserts of Midian, God revealed Himself to the man who one day would be the greatest leader Israel has ever known. Hearing the divine plan and purpose for his life, Moses posed the following question to God: *"Who am I that I should go?"* (Exodus 3:11, NASB)—a fair enough question given his personal history and reputation. In the wilderness, the former prince of Egypt no longer had a clear understanding of his person nor his position in the world. He was lost. He knew where he had been (and that seemed so distant and perplexing) but worse yet, he had no sense of where he was going. He desperately needed an identity and a role to play.

God initially ignored Moses's question and responded by giving him the name of the One who was calling him to service—*"I AM THAT I AM* (might also be translated, 'I WILL BE WHAT I WILL BE')[2] ... *The Lord, the God of your fathers"* (Exod. 3:14–15, NASB). Once Moses caught a glimpse of the Person and power of the God who beckoned him into ministry and leadership, he could better understand who he was and where he might best fit into God's plans.

Now armed with divine approval and authority, a one-time murderer, whose life was going nowhere, picked up his staff, changed course, headed back to Egypt, and boldly marched into the throne room of Pharaoh to demand the release of the Hebrew slaves. A fugitive from justice, the son of slaves, became the liberator and leader of a nation. It is a remarkable story of which D.L. Moody noted, *"Moses spent forty years thinking he was somebody; forty years learning he was nobody; and forty years discovering what God can do with a nobody."*[3]

God alone ultimately defines the pastor, ministry leader and every believer's personal identity and role in life, which first rests squarely on who God is and what He says about the man or woman who would serve Him. It is the Potter's hand that molds and shapes the individual vessel, designing each one to be suitable for a particular task and place in the world. Sometimes that journey takes a person down unusual and unchartered paths—from the barrenness of the "desert" to the steps of a palace, from a delivery boy bringing lunch to his brothers on a battle field to severing the head of a giant to secure a great victory, from a fisherman with empty nets and a career that was going nowhere to a "fisher of men" whose life would impact eternity. Identity brings transformation.

Some years later, I was asked to be the commencement speaker at a Christian college. I was deeply honored and moved by this opportunity to serve. No one would have predicted it. I later wrote to friends and family

> *Think of it—from a teenager, who stuttered and stammered so terribly, who could hardly get a word out of his mouth, who was terrified of having to speak aloud before his peers in a classroom, to a preacher and teacher, to now a commencement speaker—only God could have pulled such a thing off! I stand amazed at His grace which allowed me the privilege to serve Him in this capacity.*

The miraculous, transforming work of God in the lives of ordinary, faulty people is not an uncommon story. Many can attest to such an experience.

The prophet Samuel, a man of uncompromising faith, was assigned the task of roaming the countryside to find a specific man God would have to be the new king (cf I SAMUEL 16:1–18). He initially questioned seven applicants, all brothers and sons of Jesse—probably good men, fine men, skilled men, but none were the man God was after.

Reluctantly, they finally summoned David from the field, the youngest of the eight, who apparently was not originally on the list of acceptable candidates to be king (No one saw me as leadership or ministry material either). During his job interview with Samuel, David had little to offer. His resume was unimpressive. So was mine, I might add. Who would have guessed a shepherd boy to have the stuff necessary to sit on the throne of a nation? He was too young, too raw, and too inexperienced—just a youth, who had learned to chase sheep around the countryside for years. Yet, God saw in him what nobody else did—his heart.

When David arrived at the family tent, he was probably still stinking of sheep, sweating from the long walk home, and clothed in the rags of a herder. He was a tradesman—a blue-collar worker, who spent days in the hot sun, in the rain and mud, and was no stranger to the bitter cold nights of the region.

He wore dirty, worn Nike sandals and carried a staff in his hand, which was little more than a stick broken off from a tree. Strapped to his waist was a sling and a leather pouch of stones. He must have been quite a sight—a ruddy face, wide-eyed, skinny kid standing before a great prophet.

It is then that Samuel heard from God. *"This is the one!"* In the background, I can almost hear the murmuring of his brothers and neighbors, *"Are you kidding me?"*

The Lord, however, knew who He wanted and why he wanted him. Make no mistake. The opinions and wisdom of men mean nothing to God.

Samuel reached for the sacred oil and poured it ceremoniously over the head of David, and a young boy was given a new identity and approved by God to fill a particular role well beyond anything he, or anybody else for that matter, could have thought, hoped for, or imagined (I could relate to that).

An incredible, transformative story. One-minute David is out on the hills cleaning-up after sheep, and the next he is informed that one day, he would walk the halls of the palaces of Jerusalem. From shepherd to king. From the jagged rocks of the mountainside to the comfort of a king's chamber. From that day forward, David never again saw himself the same way.

Near the end of WWII, Dietrich Bonhoeffer, was imprisoned and executed in Germany for his faith. Locked in a dark cell awaiting his fate, Bonhoeffer asked one final question of himself. The answer would validate his entire life and the sacrifice he was about to make.

Who am I? This or the other?
Am I one person today, and tomorrow another?
Am I both at once? A hypocrite before others,
And before myself a contemptibly woebegone weakling?

Or is something within me still like a beaten army,
Fleeing in disorder from victory already achieved?

Who am I? They mock me, these lonely questions of mine.
Whoever I am, Thou knowest, O God, I am thine.[4]

In my early ministry days, I too desperately needed the reassurance that first and foremost, no matter what, I belonged to God. When all was said and done, despite the personal failures, weaknesses, fears, and inconsistencies in my daily life and ministry, I was His now and forevermore. That was critical for Bonhoeffer and it was/is critical for me.

Like so many, I worried most about *"being judged or measured by others (and falling short of their requirements)."*[5] What people thought about me became terribly important, which led to a frustrating, frantic search for identity. The problem was basically I had been *Lookin' for Love*[6] (acceptance, approval, and authentication) in the wrong places and from the wrong persons. I needed heaven's endorsement.

I sought for validation and personal worth by counting the people who responded to the weekly altar call (which wasn't many), the rate of church growth and Sunday school attendance, the number of yearly baptisms (denominations particularly like these stats), the size of the operating and mission budgets, the building of larger church facilities, the endorsement of denominational leaders, and the applause of church members. None of these had anything to do with my identity as a servant of Christ, particularly the church crowd whose approval was never a safe bet. Like most crowds, they were/are truly an unreliable bunch. One minute they will embrace you and the next they are running you out of town. One minute they will sing "Hosanna" and throw palm branches at your feet as you walk into the sanctuary and the next day they will nail you to the door of All Saints' Church in Wittenberg, Germany, right next to Martin Luther's 95 Theses. Consequently, I had no real idea who (which individual or group) to please and whose ministry standards and style to adopt—mine, theirs, or God's. The result was often conflict.

A man, who was a member of the pulpit committee and a leader in the first church I pastored, was not particularly supportive of the direction it was taking, and he was none too shy about letting others know of his disapproval. The church was growing and on the move. Things were rapidly changing (goals, constitution and by-laws, committees, officers, new members, etc.). A renewal was taking place. For months, following the Sunday morning services, the man vehemently voiced his opposition to anyone who would listen. He would corner people in the back of the church auditorium to "rally the troops" and gain support for his position. His actions soon became disruptive, and finally, I stepped in, pulled him aside, and said,

> *What you do outside the walls of this church is your business. What you do when you step through those front doors is mine. It is obvious that this church is not big enough for the two of us. And since I'm not leaving that leaves only one alternative. You are going.*

I was right; he was wrong. I stay; he leaves. I win; he loses. That was how I saw it. That was how I saw myself—like a spiritual Conan the Conqueror, but not as a Christlike lover of that man's soul. When I got a better handle on who I was and what God expected of me, I learned how to love that man, who in the end became one of my biggest supporters.

LifeWay Research conducted a survey of 734 former senior pastors who left the pastorate before retirement age. The data indicated that

> *most expected conflict to arise, and it did—56 percent clashed over changes they proposed, and 54 percent say they experienced a significant personal attack. Yet nearly half (48 percent) say their training didn't prepare them to handle the people side of ministry.*[7]

Dennis Hollinger, President of Gordon-Conwell Theological Seminary, indicated that in today's world any seminary bent on successfully preparing men and women for ministry must focus on the needs of its students. He wrote

> *To minister effectively in our complex, confused world today, our students must be grounded in God's unerring Word and know how to preach and teach it. They need to know how to think theologically in the face of pressing intellectual issues from our culture. They need to have wisdom for guiding people facing hard ethical issues in society and various professions. Students need to learn from church history to deepen their personal journey and gain understanding for the contemporary church. They need to develop ministry skills in counseling, leadership, preaching, worship, and evangelism. But learning all of this must do more than merely touch their minds. Moreover, it must encompass more than the mere passing of knowledge.*[8]

Ed Stetzer agreed.

> *Many seminary programs don't even require courses on the people side—they're focused on theology, biblical languages, and preaching, which are important, but almost half of the pastors felt unprepared for dealing with the people they were preparing in seminary to lead and serve.*[9]

And so, it was with me. There was little doubt that I had the basic *"knowledge"* a good seminary education could provide, but I had yet to learn how to handle the people side of ministry, which is at the core of pastoral and ministry work. It would take several more years of trial and error in the local church setting to gain the wisdom necessary to solidify my identity and improve my ability to effectively minister to people. There were no short-cuts. Only personal experience on the field, coupled with a growing confidence in God's Word, and a sure recognition of my calling to the pastoral ministry, all of which facilitated spiritual and professional growth—something critically needed in my early years in the church when the pain and embarrassment of poor decisions and less than Christ-like actions were so evident.

There was a woman who sang in the church choir in my first pastorate. She was but one of a handful of choir members drawn from a small congregation. This was an older church building where the choir loft sat high on a platform just to the right of the pulpit. The congregation had an unrestricted view. During a traditionally structured, Sunday morning service, the choir stood to sing a hymn while the offering was being received. At the end of the anthem, I was to rise and walk to the pulpit to deliver the sermon I had prepared. I was ready and anxious to begin. There was one choir member, however, who did not share my excitement or enthusiasm. As I was approaching the pulpit, she would invariably get up from her choir chair and exit the platform in plain sight of the entire congregation. This happened repeatedly over the course of several months, and I was hurt and embarrassed by her actions. I desperately wanted her (and everybody else) to approve and recognize my preaching abilities, and when I didn't get it, I struck out in anger. I pulled her aside one morning and said, *"If I have to listen to you sing, you are going to have to listen to me preach!"* And I made that a condition for her to continue with the choir. Not surprisingly, she left the church and didn't return. I not only failed to recognize who I was (maybe to the point, who I should have been), I had no clue who she was—a person deeply loved and valued by God, simply looking for a place to serve His interests. She deserved better than I gave.

The struggle to maintain one's personal uniqueness and calling in Christ was real and continued throughout my ministry. It required a daily response to the following question, *"Shall I be my own man today, or the man others think I should be, or will I have the guts to be God's man and serve Him to His liking?"* There was (and is) no real choice in the matter. The Apostle Paul knew that he was *"set apart from his mother's womb"* and called by God's *"grace"* to preach Christ *"among the Gentiles"* (cf Gal. 1:15-16, NASB). He had his identity and he had his calling and role, and thereby understood what that meant for his ministry. *"If I were still trying to please men,"* he wrote, *"I would not be a bond-servant of Christ"* (Gal. 1:10, NASB). And therein lays the tension in ministry—please *men* (and that included me) or please *Christ*—a decision that was compounded by the multiple opinions of others.

Paul Tripp warned, *"There are only two places to look (for identity). I will either get my identity vertically, from who I am in Christ, or I will shop for it horizontally in the situations, experiences, and relationships of my daily life."*[10] No doubt, this remains a constant danger for every pastor, servant-leader, and Christ follower.

In the eyes of some, it seemed that I was *"never good enough."* Everyone sized me up as a person and as a pastor. More than a few had something to say about how I should act, speak, feel, dress, and how I should live my daily life in and out of the Christian community. Many also "knew" how the church should be run. There were no shortage of "experts" to fill the church pews. Accordingly, the pressure came from every side to conform and fit changing and sometimes conflicting pastoral roles and ministry expectations. It was overwhelming—a struggle for which I was ill prepared. I had no hint of the coming, frequent attempts to manipulate and the conflicts to follow.

There was a women's organization called the Loyal Baptist Daughters who raised money through bazaars (a garage sale of sorts) for the local church. Over the years, they had accumulated large sums of money and used that as leverage to control the church and its administrative leadership. A problem arose when I discovered that the group was selling paperback books that were boarder line pornographic. I moved to shut down the entire operation and met with the group to address the matter. I dared to suggest that there was a better way to raise the much-needed funds for the church—through tithes and offerings. I further suggested that if they spent as much time and effort winning people to the Lord as they did selling questionable merchandise, the pews would be full, and the money problems of the church would be resolved. That didn't go over well.

THE SEARCH FOR AUTHENTICITY—IDENTITY

From their perspective, I had stepped out of the pastoral role that they had defined for me. I was expected to look the other way and say little to nothing. Some believed a "real" pastor should have no backbone. He should be emotionally weak and possess a quiet, unassuming personality, seen but not heard, non-confrontational, and certainly soft-spoken—anything but militant, feisty, unafraid, and competitive. I was more the latter—more like the Peter-type, ready to grab the nearest sword when threatened and start lopping off ears. Not surprisingly, that perspective and tactic became problematic. Though I believed I had an obligation to challenge their actions, wisdom would dictate a less inflammatory tone and approach to get the results I was after. Hind sight is great.

Experience taught me that as I accepted the expectations and judgments of others, I lost self-confidence. I lost my way. My self-esteem and sense of self-worth dropped, and I was frequently depressed, discouraged, angry, and lonely (though I rarely showed any of it outwardly). The result was an inability to connect with people consistently and effectively. Inevitability, I attempted ministry behind a mask—a facade that proved to be futile. Integrity and identity demanded a different response.

The parents of a 3-year-old girl came to see me. They were interested in dedicating their child to the Lord during a Sunday morning service. The mother was a believer and had made a commitment to Christ six months prior to our meeting. Her husband, however, did not share her faith. In fact, his character was questionable, and his reputation within the community was that of a "ladies' man." There was no pretense of him being or living as a Christian. I explained that in our church tradition baby dedications were more about the parents' commitment to raising their children within the context of a Christian community and home that valued biblical principles and less about a religious ceremony that had no genuine spiritual application or impact. I explained that the dedication also included the promise of the parents to introduce their children to the Lord and to live-out their faith in their home and before the community.

In good conscience, the mother could make such a solemn commitment. Her husband would not and could not.

At this point, tensions began to rise. I could feel it, as I challenged the father about his spiritual life and life choices. He dug-in and resisted my efforts. I eventually asked him, *"How can you promise to introduce your daughter to a God you don't know?"* He did not answer but became visibly agitated. I informed the couple that I would do the dedication for the mother. The father, however, would not be allowed to participate given his current spiritual state and lifestyle. To do otherwise, I explained, would turn a sacred moment into a meaningless religious ritual, something I was determined not to do. I was committed to biblical truth and to honor and please God before pleasing others and stood ready to uphold the sanctity and traditions of the church regardless of the pressures to do otherwise or what the personal and professional costs might be. Subsequently, the man stormed out of my office. I never saw him again.

Amid the conflict and turmoil, however, was the knowledge and the assurance of God's anointing and endorsement that stabilized my ministry and secured my sense of identity and calling. Some days I often hung by my fingernails to this simple yet profound truth that kept me in the ministry and sanctified my life. I belonged to God. I was His servant to care for His people, His ambassador to the world, and His messenger, whose primary duty was to uncompromisingly declare God's Word to those *"dead"* in their *"trespasses and sins"* (cf Eph. 2:1) and who needed to hear from Him. When I accepted the significance of that role, I was more likely to face moral and spiritual responsibilities with greater courage and conviction.

Settling the question of identity and calling is vitally important to a successful, vibrant ministry because it deepens and enlarges the faith of the pastor, ministry leader, and layperson, and produces the guts necessary to live and serve fearlessly. It was a good lesson to learn—a lesson which tested strength of character and often came by way of painful, challenging experiences, not found in a textbook or the safe surroundings of a college or seminary campus.

The Apostle Paul endured hardships, imprisonment, and repeated beatings because he understood who he was—*"a prisoner of Christ Jesus"* (Phil. 1:1), *"a bond-servant of God,"* (Titus 1:1), and *"an apostle (not sent from men, nor through the agency of man, but through Jesus Christ"* (Gal. 1:1, NASB). He was under divine orders—a man sent to his generation, to a particular place, to do a specific task, *"according to the commandment of God"* (I Tim. 1:1) and *"by the will of God"* (Col. 1:1, Eph. 1:1). That sense of calling and identity (God's man, in God's place, in God's time) kept me stubbornly focused on the divine mission before me. I knew who I was and what God wanted me to do, and with that came confidence (not arrogance) to 'stay the course' and lean fully on God's Word and will for direction and guidance. I was free to leave the *"old man"* behind and *"put on the new man"* (cf Col. 3:9–10).

C. S. Lewis stated,

> *The more we get what we now call <u>'ourselves' out of the way and let Him (God) take us over, the more truly ourselves we become.</u> The more I resist Him and try to live on my own, the more I become dominated by my own heredity and upbringing and surroundings and natural desires… It is when I turn to Christ, when I give myself up to His Personality, that I first begin to have a real personality of my own.*[11]

And therein lays the secret—getting myself *"out of the way,"* to be who Christ said I am, to do what Christ said I must do.

The bearded lady in the hit movie, *The Greatest Showman* (20th Century Fox, Dec. 2018), suffered debilitating depression and despair from years of ridicule and rejection. But all that changed when she understood herself to be a unique, important, exceptional person full of potential and promise, born to fulfill a specific place, role, and task in this world. Only then was she able to sing, *"This is Me."*[12]

There is nothing more real and freeing than that!

THE PINNACLE

"Thou hast kept my soul from the pit of nothingness…"
(Isaiah 38:17).

A dark
Foreboding place.
Empty and void…
"Nothingness."
A life entombed in
Wasted energies,
   Unproductive schedules,
      Undetermined, meaningless plans.
The decisions of a fool.
It is life without You, Lord.
The wages of sin.

But salvation came.
The Cross.
Divine mercy.
And Resurrection.
Raised from the dead in the likeness of Christ!
A new life!
A new identity!
Transformed
  By Calvary's love
  To reveal
    The splendor of human significance.
Heaven's most glorious achievement.

Wondrously,

Thankfully,
    Supernaturally
You, O LORD, made me SOMEBODY.
Somebody
    Unique.
        Special.
            Gifted by the Spirit.
To climb higher,
And upward
And out
    From the "pit of nothingness"
To live at The Pinnacle of all creation.
A son of God
His masterpiece (Eph 2:10, NLT),
Useful.
Purposeful.
Serving.
Fitting into
    Your perfect scheme.

"It is the living who gives thanks to Thee, as I do today" (Isa 38:19, NASB).

~ Sandy

... let us run with endurance the race that is set before us, fixing our eyes on Jesus, the author and perfecter of faith, who for the joy set before Him endured the cross, despising the shame, and has sat down at the right hand of the throne of God. For consider Him who has endured such hostility by sinners against Himself, so that you will not grow weary ᵇand lose heart (Hebrews 12:1–3, NASB).

CHAPTER 8
THE SURPRISE OF MINISTRY—JOY

I never gave it much thought while in the pastorate—*"What is so good about being a pastor anyway?"* No matter what I did or didn't do, the lives of so many remained in shambles. At first, I wanted and expected to see at least some measure of good come from my pastoral efforts, but I saw little of it. Consequently, the ministry became joyless and miserable. Unlike Jesus, I missed *"the joy set before* me.*"* I wanted results and I wanted them now.

The pastoral ministry (as well as other forms of service) deals mostly with human adversity. It is hard to miss—illness, death, divorce, infidelity, hopelessness, etc. I would estimate that ninety plus percent of the phone calls that came into the parsonage and church office were negative in nature. Crisis seemed to be the norm, a fact overwhelmingly evident in my formative ministry days. *"Healthy people don't need a doctor--sick people do"* (Mark 2:17, NLT).

Eugene Peterson said of his own pastoral ministry experience,

> In running a church, I solve problems. Wherever two or three are gathered together, problems develop. Egos are bruised, procedures get snarled, arrangements become confused, plans go awry.

THE SURPRISE OF MINISTRY—JOY

Temperaments clash. There are polity problems, marriage problems, work problems, child problems, committee problems, emotional problems…The difficulty is that problems arrive in such a constant flow that problem solving becomes a full-time work.[1]

Peterson was right. There was little time for much else other than dealing with a steady stream of people entangled in a series of never-ending, chaotic, destructive life patterns and tragic events. The ministry was like spinning plates at a carnival side show. I got the first plate up and moving, ran to the next, repeated my efforts, and then moved on to another. By the time the end of the line was reached, and the last plate was successfully up and spinning, I had to hurry back to where I started and do it all over again because the first plate was losing power and momentum. It was a frustrating, exhausting cycle and it never seemed to end—little progress, little victory, little satisfaction, little joy. My soul so desperately prayed and longed for *"the oil of gladness instead of mourning, the mantle of praise instead of a spirit of fainting"* (Isaiah 61:3, NASB). As I walked through the halls of the church and down the streets of the local community, I searched for a reason, any reason, to *"rejoice greatly in the Lord"* (Isaiah 61:10, NASB), something that proved unfamiliar and elusive (to say the least) in my ministry experience. It wasn't long before my prayer for some measure of joy was answered, and it came in the form of an unexpected, heart-rending, late-night call from John, one of my parishioners.

The call was one of those that none of us would ever want to make or get. He said, *"Pastor, my son was killed in a car accident a few hours ago. He was on the way home, lost control of the car… and died."* His son was 16 years old.

Early the next morning I visited John and his family. He was seated alone on his couch, head down, shoulders slumped forward. He slowly raised his head and I saw his eyes, red and nearly swollen shut. He had been up most of the night crying.

He looked at me through those tear-filled eyes and said something profoundly insightful and powerful. Sobbing, he whispered, *"I never knew how much it cost God for my salvation before this night."* And he broke down and wept more. Who wouldn't? We cried together.

Amazingly, amidst all that heartache, agony, and confusion, John saw the Cross and the grace of God more clearly than he (or I) had ever seen it before. A tragic loss caused him to comprehend the high cost of redemption and the *"breadth and length and height and depth"* (Eph.3:18, NASB) of God's love demonstrated at Calvary on his (and my) behalf. John identified with God's loss of His *"only begotten son"* (John 3:16, NASB), a precious son who was *"crushed for our iniquities"* (Isaiah 53:5, NASB). In the lowest of moments, a bruised, finite man grasped not only the story of redemption but also the most incredible theological truth upon which all of Christianity rests. The Incarnation.

Clothed in human flesh, God became *"a man of sorrows and acquainted with grief"* (Isaiah 53:3, NASB), knowing human misery, despair, and loneliness. God felt the deepest agony of a father's loss, and so did John. In the moments that followed the accident, a grieving father reached-out and touched heaven, weeping in the presence of God, acutely aware of the promise of God's redemptive action in all of this.

Intellectually, I had a handle on the Incarnation and the theology that surrounds it. Seminary taught me that much. But to *feel* the Incarnation, and to *experience* firsthand its power to transcend human tragedy was an entirely different matter.

I saw hope rise from the ashes of despair. And strangely enough, John seemed content and at peace through it all—hurting, yes, but satisfied with God's ultimate response to his heartbreak. Before my eyes and much to my amazement, the man became a *"living letter"* that testified to the miraculous, a broken heart overflowing with a joy that defied any rational explanation. I was (if I can borrow from C.S. Lewis), "surprised by joy," overwhelmed, feeling privileged to have watched this supernatural transformation take place, and thankful to God for the lessons that a father who lost his son taught me. I left John's home encouraged and glad to have had a small part to play. It was a powerful experience that changed my perspective.

There is, of course, a lighter side to ministry. It's not always so dramatic. It was three-thirty in the morning when a church member pounded loudly on my front door. He was visibly upset, trembling, and breathing heavily.

I asked him, *"What's happened? What's wrong."*

He yelled, *"She won't do it with me anymore!"*

I asked for clarification, *"What? What are you talking about?"*

Shaking his clenched fist in the air, he repeated his initial comment, *"She won't do it with me anymore!"*

He was angry and humiliated because his wife refused him intimacy and so he stormed out of their house. Apparently, this had been going on for some time and he had reached a breaking point. Rejection hurts. So, I invited him in and we sat in my study and talked for nearly two hours about his relationship with his wife. At the time, I struggled to find the humor in any of this, except that I hardly expected to be in my bathrobe having a "sex talk" with one of my parishioners in the wee hours of the morning! Looking back on the situation, I smile, convinced that God must have a sense of humor! I believe He does.

The task of ministry, however, is serious business, as every servant of God knows. Ministry is servanthood. It is selfless, generous, and deliberate action that focuses on the spiritual care of those trying to live out their daily lives as best they can. Ministry is theology with hands and feet (orthopraxis), the practical, compassionate extension of God's love, grace, and mercy to a troubled world. Ministry is helping others develop an authentic faith that works, to be reconciled with God (II Cor. 5:18), to maintain an intimate relationship with the Savior, to grow in the grace and knowledge of Christ, and to find peace and joy in a world that knows little of either.

David Tripp observed that

Personal ministry is not about always knowing what to say. It is not about fixing everything in sight that is broken. Personal ministry is about connecting people with Christ so that they are able to think as he would have them think, desire what he says is best, and do what he calls them to do even if their circumstances never get 'fixed.' It is about exposing hurt, lost, and confused people to God's glory, so that they give up their pursuit of their own glory and live for his. It is about so thoroughly embedding people's personal stories in the larger story of redemption that they approach every situation and relationship with a 'God's story' mentality. We need to be filled with awe at what the Lord has called us to participate in! ... Biblical personal ministry is more about perspective, identity, and calling than about fixing what is broken.[2]

While serving as the pastor of a local church, I took on an unusual community ministry opportunity for which I was well suited—the head boys varsity soccer coach at the local public high school. I had a successful collegiate background in the game and was confident in my ability to make a difference not only in the program that had been unproductive for many years, but more importantly in the lives of those boys who would be playing for me. In a small town, a successful high school athletic program is vitally important, because the community often rallies around their sports teams from which they draw their identity and pride. I saw this coaching position as a potential platform from which to minister and share the life-transforming message of the Gospel—and it proved to be just that.

My first day on the field I met a young man, who was a rising senior, telling the former coach that he was not medically cleared to play. Apparently, his blood work came back with a negative report that grounded him from further participation until the matter was resolved.

I walked up to him and introduced myself and said, "I could not help but over hear your conversation with coach. What's going on?"

He verified the information and reiterated his disappointment that he might not be able to play his senior year. I waited until he finished and put my hand on his shoulder and whispered, *"Son, I know a God who can heal you. I will be praying for you."*

He jumped back. You would have thought that I had touched him with a cattle prod. Eventually, the medical restriction was removed, and he was able to play out his final season. That short conversation started a relationship with the young man. He did not attend church anywhere, but over the course of several months he came frequently to my home where we talked and played ping pong. I drove him home one night and as he stepped out of the car, he turned and said to me, *"You are not like any minister I have ever met before."* I smiled, thanked him, and told him it was the best compliment anyone had ever paid me.

One afternoon following a spirited game of table tennis he asked me, *"Coach, Tell me about your faith. Why do you believe like you do?"*

This was the moment I had been waiting for—an opportunity to share the Gospel. We talked. He listened. I prayed that God would open his mind and heart to the message of the Cross. I told him I didn't want him to make any decisions at this point, but to go home and think about what I had said, and we would meet and speak again. He said he would.

Four hours later, he called me.

"Coach!"

"Yes!".

"I did it."

"What did you do?"

"I did just what you told me to do. I asked Jesus into my heart."

"And then what?" I was looking for confirmation, and I got it.

He said, *"I went into my bedroom and pulled out all the booze and drugs from my dresser draw and flushed them down the toilet."*

I knew that something (or Someone) had changed that boy's heart. It was rumored that he may have been selling drugs to his friends and was a frequent user himself. It was the primary reason he nearly lost his senior year on the team. But he didn't. God healed him inside and out.

Miraculously, the young man graduated from the state university, having completed his computer science degree in three years and was later admitted to seminary for theological training. To this day, I still rejoice over what God had done and for the part He permitted me to play in that boy's life. I had gotten a taste of the magnitude and excitement that comes with being used of God—a joy that exceeds expectations and often extends beyond the four walls of the church.

Unfortunately, several members of the congregation gave me a difficult time over my involvement in the local school system, where I had the privilege of ministering the grace of God to several hurting kids. One was near suicide after losing both her parents and another was admitted to the psych ward for drug related hallucinations. I may have never known those troubled teens had I listened to the critics and stayed locked away within the walls of the church.

The complaint over my involvement in the community was certainly shortsighted and blatantly self-centered. Some church members reasoned, *"What are we paying him for? To serve the schools? He is supposed to be working for us!"* But I ignored their complaints, continued my ministry, and became the unofficial chaplain for some of the school district's faculty, staff, and students.

For example, the mother of one of my student-athletes had taken ill and was rushed to the local hospital for emergency surgery. When checking-in to the medical facility, the hospital staff asked her if she wanted them to call her priest (She had a Catholic background).

She said, *"No!"*

The in-take staff person asked, *"So, who do you want me to call?"*

The woman said, *"I want you to call my son's soccer coach!"*

We laughed later about how that may have sounded.

Shortly thereafter, I was notified of her hospital admission and drove to the facility. Neither she or her husband were members of the church I pastored but having built a relationship with the family over a four-year period, I was afforded the opportunity to minister and carry the mercy and hope of God to her bedside. For me, the joy of ministry was the privilege of bringing Heaven down to that hospital ward and seeing the smile and relief on that mother's face and that of her family when they realized that God could be trusted to show up in the hour of their greatest need. I learned that the joy of ministry was about standing in the gap between Heaven and Earth and carrying on the mediating work of Christ the best I could (cf John 14:12-14). It didn't get much more fulfilling or better than that.

At the final sports award banquet of the year, the father of a high school student-athlete stood to introduce me. He said something that validated my ministry efforts in the community and left me speechless and grateful, this from a man who had no Christian bias or axe to grind. I have never forgotten his words. He said, "*Most of you know that Coach Z is also a minister, but I want to tell you that he has been successful at taking <u>the ministry out of the church and bringing it to the community.</u> He has shown us what church is all about. And for that we are very thankful.*"

So was I—not just for the recognition and affirmation, but for the sheer joy of having invested in the lives of people. There is nothing quite like it.

Ministry opportunities are everywhere and not limited to formal pastoral work. D.L. Mayfield, who has worked with refugee communities for nearly 10 years, concluded

> *Some of the most unrecognized ministries are my favorite kind.*
>
> *Like the ministry of playing video games with awkward adolescent boys (or ping pong). The ministry of bringing takeout food to people whose baby is very sick in the hospital. The ministry of picking up empty chip wrappers at the park. The ministry of sending postcards. The ministry of sitting in silence with someone in the psych ward. The ministry of sending hilarious and inspirational text messages. The ministry of washing dishes without being asked. The ministry of flower gardening. The ministry of not laughing at teenagers when they talk about their relationship crises. The ministry of making an excellent cup of coffee. The ministry of drinking a terrible cup of*

coffee with a bright smile. The ministry of noticing beauty everywhere—in fabrics, in art, and in the wilderness... ...more and more I am hearing the still small voice calling me to be the witness. To live in proximity to pain and suffering and injustice instead of high-tailing it to a more calm and isolated life. To live with eyes wide open on the edges of world, the margins of our society. To taste the diaspora, the longing, the suffering, the joy. To plant myself in a place where I am forced to confront the fact that my reality is not the reality of my neighbors. And to realize that nothing is how it should be, the ultimate true reality of what God's dream for the world is... I am starting to believe in this love, with Jesus as my example. He sought out the stateless wanderers, the exiles, the people with stories so sad and unfair, the ones who were the most receptive to his message that another world was possible. He has asked me to be a witness to those same kinds of people, and in return I have experienced a faith in God that could never be taught1 (my emphasis).³

I agree. A vibrant, active faith only happens when ministry leaders and followers of Christ get their hands dirty in messy, chaotic lives and bring the message and power of the gospel into the mundane affairs of daily life. There I found joy in the practical, down-to-earth aspects of ministry, something that could not be learned in a classroom setting. Of course, that makes ministry challenging, but in the end, it produced a meaningful, highly rewarding, fulfilling, and enriching experience that some ministry leaders have unfortunately missed.

One pastor observed, *"I mourn the loss of so many seminary classmates who began the ministry journey but dropped out along the way—would that they could have appreciated these (good) elements of the work."*⁴

The good *"elements of the work"* is the surprise of ministry, that deepening sense of fulfillment and satisfaction that transcends the messiness of people's lives and provides a counterbalance to the stresses and strain of serving the local church and community. Joy comes when you

- Bring the love and mercy of God to a dying man struggling with cirrhosis of the liver due to years of alcohol abuse.
- Walk through a painful divorce with a young, despondent woman who no longer sees any hope for her future.
- Celebrate and care for people during the most important times in their lives (births, marriages, deaths, baptisms, birthdays, anniversaries, etc.)
- Stand in the hope and power of the resurrection at the gravesite of a young soldier, husband, and father, who lost a two-year battle with cancer, weeping with those who weep and rejoicing with those who one day will smile again when the *"trumpet of God"* sounds *"and the dead in Christ will rise first"* (I Thess. 4:16, NASB).
- Give a cup of cold water and a bag of groceries in the name of Jesus to a single mom with two children struggling to get by on food stamps.
- Sit in the hospital ward for hours talking and praying with a man anxiously waiting for his wife to deliver their first-born son.
- Share the hope of God while walking across an open field with a dejected, utterly despondent man who had recently returned home from work to find his wife sleeping with his best friend.
- Receive an unexpected phone call from a stranger who was looking for a place to give a much needed, unsolicited, sizeable donation to the church for tax purposes.
- Work together side-by-side with other men, digging in rocky soil to prepare the foundation of a new church building.
- Play softball and talk "trash" at a church picnic.
- Study and proclaim the life-giving message of the Word of God.
- Teach and train believers for *"the work of ministry"* and then watch them succeed in their place of service in God's kingdom.
- See God miraculously answer the prayers of His people for the healing of a cancer patient who was given little hope of recovery.

- Hold the hand of a ninety-three-year-old woman confined to a nursing home and alone in this world, as she tells you her "story" of a life that has passed all too quickly.

It became abundantly clear that contentment and joy in ministry would have to be found beyond the "numbers," which was quite disconcerting for a ministry leader like myself who initially measured his success solely on the basis outcomes. There had to be a better way and I saw it in the ministry of the prophet Isaiah. His response to God's call served as an example for me and remains a model for every pastor and follower of Christ.

Isaiah was commissioned to carry God's demands for repentance to a wayward Judah and challenge the religious crowd and the cultural norms of his day. At first, it may have seemed like a pretty good gig, a spokesperson for *"the Lord, high and exalted"* (Isaiah 6:1, NIV). It was a prestigious job title by most any standard. But there were no available, training classes for prophets. No formal, "temple" lectures. Nothing available to teach him in that single, defining moment how to respond appropriately to the divine call and confidently press forward into God's business. He was not moved by proper doctrine, denominational distinctives, synagogue notes, a good Bible commentary, or by the latest translations of the Torah, but by an intimate encounter with the living God. He had *"seen the King, the Lord of hosts"* (Isaiah 6:5), and it changed his life and perspective. It should have! He had but one option: *"Here am I. Send me!"* (Isaiah 6:8, NASB). Frankly, not much else needed to be said in response. No stuttering. No stammering. No thinking it over. No question. He was going to work for the King. This was the opportunity of a lifetime and Isaiah immediately stepped up to the challenge and was ready to accept the divine assignment without fully knowing what he was supposed to be doing or where his ministry would take him. Subsequently, the man got his marching orders and received clear and concise instructions from the Throne. *"Go and tell the people."* Tell them to stop playing the spiritual *"harlot"* (cf Isaiah 1:21). Call them to repentance. Demand righteous living and obedience.

There was one additional fact, however, God wanted Isaiah to know before he got started. The ears of the people would be *"dull"* (cf Isaiah 6:9–10). No one would *"understand."* No one would take him seriously. No one would affirm him or encourage him. No one would pat his back and say, *"Good message today, pastor!"* So, Isaiah asked the obvious, *"Lord, how long?"* (Isaiah 6:11), a question asked many times over by many a servant.

The prophet spent the next fifty to sixty years preaching without a single convert that we know of to his credit. By human standards, he had an unrewarding, unfulfilling, and thankless job, which meant that he would have to find joy and fulfillment elsewhere in his ministry (like so many of us). In the end, servanthood, commitment, obedience, and faithfulness would be his only motivation. And so, it was for me. These were and are the key components to a successful, fulfilling ministry, a noteworthy lesson taught outside formal, professional training.

Satisfaction does not always come in visible, concrete ways but in the willingness and determination to *"faithfully and wholeheartedly in the fear of the LORD"* (II Chronicles 19:9, NIV) do what God has called a person to do. Isaiah could never take comfort in the number of converts (baptisms and church growth statistics) notched on the binding of his scrolls, but in the simple act of obedience in fully carrying out God's assignments. The results of his ministry were to be left with God and that principle he (and I) found to be enough.

On September 4, 1869, Hudson Taylor, the man who opened China to the gospel, received a letter from John McCarthy (friend & colleague) that would later change his entire outlook on his life and ministry. The letter served to prepare Taylor for the most difficult year of his life. By the summer of 1870, he buried two sons (Samuel and Noel) and grieved over the loss of his wife (Maria) to cholera. She was thirty-three years old, leaving Hudson with four children to raise.[5] Hudson remembered his friend's letter and wrote

When my agony of soul was at its height, a sentence in a letter from dear McCarthy was used to remove the scales from my eyes, and the Spirit of God revealed to me the truth of our oneness with Jesus as I had never known it before. The prayer of Ephesians 1:18 was answered as never before: 'having the eyes of your hearts enlightened, that you may know…' As I read, I saw it all!… I looked to Jesus and saw (and when I saw, oh, how joy flowed!) that He had said, 'I will never leave thee.'"

I saw not only that Jesus will never leave me, but that I am a member of His body, of His flesh and of His bones. The vine is not the root merely, but all—root, stem, branches, twigs, leaves, flowers, fruit. And Jesus is not that alone—He is soil and sunshine, air and showers, and ten thousand times more than we have ever dreamed, wished for, or needed. Oh, the joy of seeing this truth!…

How to get faith (joy) strengthened? Not by striving after faith (or by striving after joy), but by resting on the Faithful One.[6]

The key to joy in my own ministry amid the most difficult of circumstances was learning to rest daily and simply on Jesus, *"the Faithful One."* Knowing the constancy and trustworthiness of God is a critical factor in life and ministry, especially when the soul is in agony. *"Joy"* does come *"in the morning"* (Psalm 30:5, NASB), as God proves Himself again and again over the long haul. Count on it. That lesson, however, does not come easily or quickly.

It took Elisha Hoffman twenty-five years of ministry experience in the local church to finally pen one of the most important lessons he had ever learned: *"What a joy divine… what a peace is mine, leaning on the everlasting arms."*[7] As the years past, I too began to rely more and more on the Person, power, and provision of Christ, whether my labors were going well or they were producing little, visible results. Either way, I simply set my attention squarely on Christ and nowhere else. That was enough. He was enough, and that helped to settle an anxious heart.

Anne Graham Lotz spent years traveling the world teaching the Word of God yet struggled with family difficulties and personal loss that threatened her ministry effectiveness. In an interview, she put things in perspective for every servant-leader. She said, *"In the midst of the stress, pressure, and weariness, I knew I didn't want to quit ministry or to escape life; I didn't want a vacation. I didn't even ask God for a miracle. The cry of my heart was, 'Just give me Jesus...'"* [8]

I got the message—*"Just give me Jesus."* Clearly, I needed Him to find joy in what I was doing.

While serving in the local church and looking for answers to a troubling ministry, I came across a book (besides the Bible, of course) that had a tremendous impact on my life and service. It was A.W. Tozer's, *The Knowledge of the Holy*, a powerful, insightful work that touched my soul, challenged my thinking, lifted my spirit, and changed my perspective about God, myself, and the ministry. The first time I read that book in those early days of serving the local church, I broke down and wept as I sat in my study alone with God and considered anew the very character of the One who has made Heaven His throne and Earth His footstool (cf Isa. 66:1). Frankly, I needed an encounter with *The Holy*, and got it through the truth contained in the pages of that book. Every word seemed like a "transfiguration" (cf Luke 17:1–8) experience that gave me a fresh glimpse of the Savior and produced a new measure of courage and hope in the future of my ministry and a deep sense of joy about the God I was called to serve.

In 1918, Helen Howarth Lemmel published one of the great hymns of the church, *The Heavenly Vision*. The words of that song were inspired by a pamphlet entitled (most appropriately) *Focused*, and written by the missionary, Isabella Lilias Trotter,[9] who worked with the "prostitutes of Victoria Station" in London and the YMCA.[10] The first two lines of the chorus of Lemmel's hymn sets forth the only method and means for every pastor and ministry leader (in fact, any person) to find genuine joy in their life and service to the kingdom of God.

> *Turn your eyes upon Jesus*
> *Look full in His wonderful face*
> *And the things of earth will grow strangely dim*
> *In the light of His glory and grace*

That principle may have been the most important lesson I ever learned in those early ministry days and it has sustained me over the years. *"Consider Him... so that you will not grow weary and lose heart"* (Hebrews 12:1-3, NASB). He is and remains the *"joy set before"* me!

"I longed to be as a flame of fire, continually glowing in the divine service, preaching, and building up Christ's Kingdom, to my latest, my dying moment... I felt now the same freedom in prayer for the people of my charge, for the propagation of the Gospel among the Indians, and for the enlargement of Zion in general... and longed to burn out in one continual flame for God."[1] ~ David Brainerd

CHAPTER 9
THE CALL TO DUTY & RESPONSIBILITY—THE CHARGE

I remember the day I accepted the call to my first church. It was both exhilarating and frightening. I was excited but also disquieted and fearful of heart. Like a marriage the ministry (any ministry) should never be entered into *"unadvisedly, but soberly, reverently, and in the fear of God."* I knew that I was about to take on the heavy responsibilities of ministry. I just didn't know how heavy that load would be.

Regardless, "play time" was over. This was about to get real—real people, real problems, real ministry. And I was not at all comfortable with that prospect. Frankly, nobody should be. The thought of engaging in hands-on ministry and fulfilling the role of a pastor and serve the needs of people with any degree of competency was incredibly intimidating. I was agonizingly aware of my own limitations and inadequacies for the task ahead, and I wasn't ready. I admit it.

Anticipating my first ministry assignment, I thought to myself, *"These church people actually expect me to be knowledgeable and competent."* But I knew otherwise, and before I took my first step through the doors of the local church, I already had begun to question my ability to direct and sustain a successful ministry. I was scared, knowing that the spiritual health and effectiveness of the church and its members would soon be resting in my incompetent and ill-prepared hands. A good education didn't help much either to quiet my fears. It simply showed me just how much I didn't know, which was painfully confirmed in the months ahead.

The demands of service and servanthood are high and the expectations for kingdom workers are even higher. A greater *"judgment,"* wrote James, awaits a *"teacher,"* one whose primary duty is to instruct the church and clarify the meaning and application of God's word, certainly a major task for the pastor-teacher and ministry leader (cf James 3:1, NASB).

The only exception to the rule (a little sarcasm here) may be those few, courageous souls destined to tend the nursery or teach the pre-school class in the local church. They are, in fact, a breed set apart from the norm whose reward in Heaven will be great for having to deal with screaming infants, teething babies, lost pacifiers, dirty diapers, and hair-pulling, highly demanding toddlers who can't sit still or keep their hands to themselves! God bless those people for serving!

Seriously, the requirements for discipleship and for all servants of Christ begin with a stern warning to *"count the cost"* (Luke 14:28, NASB) before one attempts to build a life as a true follower, establish a ministry to meet the needs of people, or enter the spiritual battle for the souls of men and women. The weight of that responsibility and the preparation needed (formal and otherwise) to do the job right dare not be ignored or lessened. The call of God demands our very best on all fronts, a lesson learned early on in my ministry.

My initial introduction to pastoral duty and responsibility came at the hands of a seasoned pastor who bragged to me at a community, ministerial meeting that he spent little to no time preparing for his Sunday morning sermon. He said

> *Sometimes I might sit down on Saturday night and think about what I want to say the next morning, but most of the time I just come to the pulpit without much forethought and simply say whatever comes to mind."*

He was quite serious.

He then asked, *"How much time do you spend?"*

I responded, *"Fifteen to twenty hours per week."*

He laughed, *"Oh, you'll get over that."* And walked away.

Frankly, I was stunned and wondered what the man did all day if he wasn't reading, studying, praying, and preparing for the most important hour of the week? It was his responsibility to stand before the people and in the name of the King of kings, *"the everlasting God, the Lord, the creator of the ends of the earth"* (Isa. 40:28, NASB) speak forth the *"wonderful words of life"*[2] to a dying world that needs to hear from God. The most sobering of all divine assignments is to boldly declare, *"Thus says the Lord"* (Jere. 9:23–24; Ezekiel 11:5, NASB) and do it with conviction and humility. Few get that privilege or opportunity. For days I thought about the lack of integrity exemplified by that particular pastor and the total disregard, disrespect, and contempt for the call of God upon his life, the word of God, and for the people he was divinely commissioned to serve. He should have known better. He should have done better. Subsequently, I clearly saw what I didn't want for my ministry and came away from that experience thankful to God for teaching an important lesson that would serve me the rest of my career.

What I needed then (and still do) was to feel the full weight of divine service and the accompanying duties and responsibilities that come with such a sacred undertaking. The weightiness of those tasks kept me humble, dependent upon God and focused on doing and being my best. That perspective was the difference between succeeding or failing in the mundane routines of daily ministry.

NFL legend, Vince Lombardi, entered the locker room for his first team meeting with the Green Bay Packers, who had finished their previous season with a dismal 1-11 record—a less than impressive performance. It was 1959 and the team had gathered to meet their new coach. Little did they know the cultural change from losers to winners that was about to take place. The men were quietly seated in their locker room, anxiously awaiting Lombardi's arrival.

Finally, the coach stepped through the door and made his way into the room. He stopped, gazed into the eyes of his players, and announced the secret to their future success—the one guiding principle that would take the team from the bottom of the NFL to the heights of Super Bowl Sunday.

> *Gentlemen, we are going to relentlessly chase perfection, knowing full well we will not catch it, because nothing is perfect. But we are going to relentlessly chase it, because in the process we will catch excellence. I am not remotely interested in just being good.*[3]

Neither was I.

Later, Lombardi was heard to say, *"You don't do things right once in a while… you do them right all the time."*[4] Not surprisingly, he turned the Packers into champions because he insisted on self-discipline, persistence, dedication, loyalty, and personal accountability. He demanded that every team member, player and coach alike, meet their respective duties and responsibilities on and off the field and carry out their assignments to the best of their ability. No excuses. No nonsense. Just get the job done right, first time, every time. The results speak for themselves. The Super Bowl trophy bears the Lombardi name, as it should. Excellence pays dividends.

Excellence is the best *in* me, the best *of* me, and the best *from* me in the efforts I make and the attitudes I maintain in fulfilling all that God has called me (or any person) to be and to do. And that includes not just the athletic field, but also the classroom, the corporate board room, the family home, the community soup kitchen, or in the church. Everyone. Everything. Everywhere. Excellence brings vibrancy and victory in life and ministry. Conversely, lack luster performance and half-hearted attempts at doing God's work (or any work for that matter) are profoundly irresponsible and irreverent and will most certainly result in failed, unproductive ministries. Mediocrity is simply not good enough. It never has been, not for the King.

Admiral Hyman Rickover asked Jimmy Carter about his academic standing at the Naval Academy. Carter replied that he had finished 59th in his class of 820. Rickover pressed Carter further, and asked, *"Did you do your best?"* Carter admitted that he had not. The admiral posed one final question, and it pierced the heart of a young naval officer wanting to serve his country. Rickover asked, *"Why not?"*[5] Lesson learned. "The harder I work, the luckier I get!"[6]

Excellence is the key to success in life and ministry, requiring servant-leaders to sell out daily and completely to Christ and His work, and thus *"walk in a manner worthy of the Lord, to please Him in all respects, bearing fruit in every good work"* (Col. 1:10). In other words, chase *"perfection,"* not in hopes of ever achieving such levels, but with the goal to "catch excellence" along the way. Such effort honors the God who calls and equips every believer and ministry leader alike to be more than mediocre. The best efforts produce the best results.

The single, most important requirement for serving God, regardless of the field or place of ministry, is the desire to give (in the words of Oswald Chambers) *My Utmost for His Highest*—the total and wholehearted surrender of talents, skills, resources, attitude, personal agenda, actions, ambitions, and much more, to the will of the Master. Nothing held back. The call of God to serve in any capacity carries a high level of responsibility, and ministry done on a lesser plain mocks and cheapens that calling. Ministry is too important and sacred to be tossed away as insignificant and unworthy of great effort.

The Apostle Paul set the standard for every pastor, ministry-leader, and layperson. To the best of his God-given ability, Paul carried out his mission with fervency and conviction, and preached *"Christ crucified, to Jews a stumbling block, and to Gentiles foolishness"* (I Cor. 2:23, NASB). He was relentless in his divinely appointed work. *"Woe is me,"* said Paul, *"if I don't preach the gospel"* (I Cor. 9:16, NASB). Ministry must bring out the very best in every servant of God, though tragically, it is not always evident or eagerly pursued.

Following a mid-week prayer service, a fifteen-year-old boy informed me that several men, who were passing through the local community, had recently "prophesized over him" at a neighboring church and told him that he was destined to be a "great Bible teacher." Naturally, the young man was excited and waited for my approval and encouragement.

I immediately asked, *"Great! Where are you going to school?"*

He said, *"I'm not. I don't have to go. God will teach me what I need to know and tell me what I need to say."*

I responded,

Son, I'm not saying that God can't do that, but that seems to be the exception to the rule and not the norm. There are few D.L Moody's in this world. The responsibilities and duties of ministry, particularly teaching the word of God, requires the best preparation you can get to adequately meet the demands of the task. Preparation is critical. Let me remind you that Jesus spent 30 of his 33 years preparing for a three-year ministry that rocked eternity. Maybe you should consider following His example.

He didn't. No preparation. No sense of duty and responsibility. No ministry of any consequence. *"The price of greatness,"* said Winston Churchill, *"is responsibility."*[7]

One of my students once wrote of his pastor, *"His sermons are the same; there is no spark… I long for so much more."* God help those of us, who are tasked with preaching/teaching His word, to do better—that our words may actually bring genuine life and hope to hearers and not subject them to a slow tortuous death Sunday after Sunday. Serving the local church is a holy task, deserving better than that.

I recall the night when just three people showed up for the evening service. Two of the three were elderly women (Blanche and Beatty) who had walked with God for many years and were faithful church members. I had spent hours praying and studying, pouring over my Greek text and an assortment of Bible commentaries in preparing for the evening. I was ready. I had done my homework, and I felt good about it. Concerned that I might succumb to discouragement over the poor turn-out, those dear ladies pulled me aside said, *"Pastor, keep doing what you're doing. We're praying and we have a good feeling about you and what's happening in this church. Don't worry about this evening. You're doing a good job. Stay at it. Change will come."* That challenged me and forced me to ask myself one important question, *"Would I be as faithful in proclaiming the word of God to three people as I would be if I was preaching to three thousand?"* The question demanded a firm response. The answer would get to the heart of the matter. Was I was willing to shoulder the responsibilities and duties that came with serving God? I needed to know.

A.W. Tozer, without the benefit of Bible school training, was appointed pastor of the Alliance church in Nutter Fork, West Virginia. Following his ordination into the Christian ministry in August of 1920, he talked with God in solitude and secret as he considered the weightiness of what lay ahead. Though inexperienced, Tozer already had a firm and profound understanding of his call to the ministry and the accompanying responsibilities that came with service to the King and the local church. And so he humbly prayed

> "O Lord, I have heard Thy voice and was afraid. Thou hast called me to an awesome task in a grave and perilous hour… O Lord, my Lord, Thou hast stooped to honor me to be Thy servant. No man taketh this honor upon himself save he that is called of God as was Aaron. Thou has ordained me Thy messenger to them that are stubborn of heart and hard of hearing. They have rejected Thee, the Master, and it is not to be expected that they will receive me, the servant.
>
> My God, I shall not waste time deploring my weakness nor my unfittedness for the work. The responsibility is not mine, but Thine. Thou hast said, 'I knew thee—I ordained thee—I sanctified thee,' and Thou hast also said, 'Thou shalt go to all that I shall send thee, and whatsoever I command thee thou shalt speak.' Who am I to argue with

Thee or to call into question Thy sovereign choice? The decision is not mine but Thine. So be it, Lord. Thy will, not mine, be done…

I accept hard work and small rewards in this life. I ask for no easy place. I shall try to be blind to the little ways that could make life easier… And now, O Lord of heaven and earth, I consecrate my remaining days to Thee; let them be many or few, as Thou wilt. Let me stand before the great or minister to the poor and lowly; that choice is not mine and I would not influence it if I could. I am Thy servant to do Thy will, and that will is sweeter to me than position or riches or fame and I choose it above all things on earth or in heaven.

Though I am chosen of Thee and honored by a high and holy calling, let me never forget that I am but a man of dust and ashes, a man with all the natural faults and passions that plague the race of men. I pray Thee, therefore, my Lord and Redeemer, save me from myself while trying to be a blessing to others. Fill me with Thy power by the Holy Spirit, and I will go in Thy strength and tell of Thy righteousness, even Thine only. I will spread abroad the message of redeeming love while my normal powers endure.

Then, dear Lord, when I am old and weary and too tired to go on, have a place ready for me above, and make me to be numbered with Thy saints in glory everlasting. Amen."[8]

Tozer deeply understood his responsibility before God as a local church pastor and ministry leader, and thus first sought the power of God to fulfill his duties honorably and effectively. He needed help, as I did (and do). Tozer saw the ministry as big, too big for any man to take lightly or handle apart from divine assistance. He was, as he said, *"a man of dust and ashes,"* like the rest of us. Thus, he prayed fervently because he knew that ministry was too challenging, too large, too important, and too vital to depend on flesh and blood alone to get the job done. Tozer suspected that his own humanity would limit his success

THE CALL TO DUTY & RESPONSIBILITY—THE CHARGE

and effectiveness. He was right, and I knew it. Whether God would send me to the back alleyways of Calcutta, to Wall Street, or to a small-town nursing home to meet a 90-year-old woman nearing the end of her life, my commitment level to kingdom service and my reliance upon God would have to rise accordingly. The *"high and holy calling of God"* demands accountability and an unwavering faith in Him for the necessary strength and fortitude to complete each divine assignment and task.

One day a neighbor asked me to visit his mother in the hospital. She was an elderly lady with severe heart problems that threatened her life. The prognosis was not good. She was dying. I went to the hospital and made my way to the ICU where the woman was hooked up to a number of monitors and an assortment of IV's slowly dripping life-sustaining fluids into her veins. She was confined to her room, clinging to life, a prisoner "chained" to a hospital bed, unable to speak or move. I made my way to her bed side and introduced myself as a friend of her son and the pastor of a local church. I said,

> *Ma'am, I've never met you before and I don't know if you know Jesus or not or have ever heard the good news of the Gospel. But I'm here to tell you of God's love for you and to bring you the hope of Heaven and eternity.*

Before I could get started, she managed to push herself up on one elbow and turn her head towards me. She couldn't respond verbally, but her eyes were aflame with hatred. In one swift, decisive motion of rejection she swung her arm defiantly and angrily clawed and raked at the air, as if to scream, *"Get out of here! Get out! I don't want to hear it. I don't want anything to do with God, nor you for that matter. Just get out and stay out!"*

Surprised, I took a step back and whispered softly

> *I'm not going anywhere, and neither are you. So, listen carefully. You are dying. This may be your last opportunity. You are going to meet God soon,*

and when you do, I want you to be prepared. You are going to hear me out. The rest is between you and the Lord. But one thing is for certain, you will not be able to stand before the Tribunal of God, as we all will someday, and say that nobody ever told you, because I'm going to tell you about the Cross and the love and grace of God and the hope of Heaven and eternity—whether you want to hear it or not.

She rolled on her side, turned her back, and defiantly faced the wall. No matter. I did what I had promised, and told her *"the old, old story of Jesus and His love,"*[9] and then quietly left the room. I don't know what happened as a result of that encounter. That was and is God's business. My duty and responsibility was merely to do what God had sent me there to do—present the Gospel and pray, leaving the Spirit of God to do His work and soften her heart, contend with her stubborn will, and bring her to Christ, *"kicking, struggling, resentful,"*[10] if need be. It is what pastors, ministry leaders, and all members of the body of Christ are supposed to do.

The following (*The Charge*) is a straightforward, no-nonsense call to duty and responsibility directed primarily at those sent out into the world with divine authority to serve faithfully and wholeheartedly as pastors in the local church. It is also applicable to all ministry leaders and workers, regardless of where they may be serving. *The Charge* is a composite and summary of the lessons learned during years of ministry. It was originally written over forty years ago as an exhortation for a young man about to enter the pastoral ministry. The principles and expectations laid out are rooted in personal experience, church history, and divine instruction. Consequently, they remain relevant to this day, confronting and charging those called of God to take seriously the sacred tasks committed to them and to motivate every *"bond-servant of God"* to stay the course and advance the Kingdom of God.

The Charge

Rise!
Take your stand!
Be counted
Among those called of God.
Set apart by Divine decree.
   Formed
     And shaped.
In eternity past.
Equipped.
Consecrated.
   Supernaturally.
      Supremely.
         Sovereignly.
By Divine wisdom and power,
To serve the interests of Heaven.

Stubbornly,
Hold firm to your calling.
Heaven has granted it.
Let no man
Nor devil
Rob you of that.
Or deny you
    Your appointed station in God's Kingdom.
That place belongs to you
   And to no one else.
Do not surrender it easily.

Go to the mighty courts of Egypt,
If that is where God sends you.
Or sink into the mud pits
With the likes of Jeremiah.
Go to the lion's den.
To the arena.
To the prisons of Rome.
Wherever…
But go!
Applauded by Heaven.
   Approved.
      Affirmed.
In the knowledge that
"I AM has sent me…"

Be like the prophets of old,
God's spokesman.
Wholly given over to
   His word.
      His will.
         His work.
           His way.
Though unfashionable,
Unfavorable,
Unpleasant,
Say what God wants said.
Without apology.
Without compromise.
Without wavering.

Resist the temptation to be admired.
To be stroked.
To be popular.
Adulation is manipulative
Subtle.
Deadly.
Don't sell out to the crowd
Confront.
    Challenge.
        Comfort.
With the Word of the Living God.
It shall not return void!

The prophets vowed,
"As the Lord lives,
What my God says,
That will I speak."
Go thou and do likewise.
No more.
No less.
In season.
Out of season.
When it's safe,
And when it's risky.
"Whether they listen or not."
Preach the Word!
Faithfully.
    Fearlessly.
        Fervently.
Dig deep into God's Word.

Be diligent!
Do your homework.
Explore.
    Experience
        Extract "the word of truth".
Handle the Scriptures well.
Accurately.
    Precisely.
        With intellectual honesty.
Emotional integrity.
Spiritual vitality.
As a skilled,
Proud "workman".

Then,
Shepherd the flock.
Responsibly.
    Reverently.
        Rightly.
It is deserving of your finest effort.
There is no higher calling.
No nobler task.
No service
Of any form
    Or substance
That measures up to
The demands,
    The pressures
        The weight
Of the shepherd's responsibilities.

For you *"keep watch"* over the souls of men.
That IS your duty.
Bear the weight of that task.
Fear the awesome Day of Accountability.
Yours is a *"stricter judgment."*
Consequently,
Extend your faith to its limits.
   Enlarge the borders of your ministry.
      Employ every talent.
         Exhaust all strength,
In the cause of Christ.
Pursue excellence!
And
When the Chief Shepherd appears,
You shall receive
The "unfading crown of glory".

However,
Be forewarned!
Neither the crown
Nor glory come cheaply.
The call of God exacts a heavy toll.
It always does.
Ask the likes of Elijah.
Ezekiel.
John the Baptist.
Paul.
You stand in good company.
But make no mistake.
The cost is high.

Your head on a platter.
   Shipwreck.
      Chains.
         The furnace.
        Thorns.
        The cross.
Someone should tell you,
"Difficult times WILL come."
Relentless problems.
Mounting, ceaseless pressures.
Unavoidable.
   Unexplainable.
      Unwanted pain.
Physical.
   Emotional.
      Spiritual.
It is doubtful whether any man can perform well
In God's service
Without being hurt,
And feeling hurt.
You need to feel.
Heartache.
   Heartbreak.
The sting of adversity.
Don't panic, though.
It's the stuff from which
Maturity is made.
Spirituality is increased.
Wisdom grows.
Sensitivity is produced.

And tolerance is gained.
Pay the price!

Resolve
To fight the good fight!
Prepare yourself
   To do battle.
Brace yourself for the
   Inevitable struggle that awaits.
You are going to war
   Against the powers of darkness.
Stationed…
   On the frontlines.
Within firing range.
Shot at.
   Shot down.
A clear target for the Enemy!
"Suffer hardship."
Good soldiers always do.
Struggles.
   Strivings.
     Sweat.
It all goes with the job.

Regardless,
Persevere *"under trial."*
The crown of life is at stake.
Retreat, if necessary,
REST.
Recuperate,

Battle fatigue is normal.
But get patched-up quickly.
Pray much!
Without ceasing.
And return to your post.
Revived **IN** the Spirit.
    Replenished **BY** the Spirit.
        Resolved **WITH** the Spirit.
To upset the Devil's plans.
And destroy the fortresses of demons.
Like Paul,
Get a mean reputation in hell.

Certainly,
Sacrifice much.
But not everything.
Some things must be saved.
Keep your integrity.
Keep your dreams
Keep *"the joy of the Lord"*.
After all, it is your strength.
And keep your family.
I beg you…
Do not sacrifice your wife or your children
Upon the altar of the ministry.
Do not pass them through the fire
Of your neglect.
Your kids are God's gift.
Take them seriously.
Be their pastor, too.

More important.
Be their dad.
   Available.
      Accessible.
         Approachable.

And your wife?
"she is worth far more than rubies".
Precious.
And priceless.
Far more than
Treasures and trophies.
Far more than
The flattering plaudits of the church crowd.
People are fickle, anyway.
One minute they will sing
"Hosanna!"
And lay palm branches at your feet.
In the next,
They will hurl insults
And nail you to a tree.
Smarten up!
Set limits for yourself.
For your marriage.
Have some guts.
Learn to say *"No!"* to the church.
And take care of your wife.
Before God
And the heavenly hosts,
I charge you

To love your wife above the church.
Before the people.
Above yourself.

Finally,
Be strong and courageous!
Be careful to do according to God's Word.
Heaven's program.
   Heaven's plan.
      Heaven's purpose.
Do not turn from it to the right
Or to the left,
So that you may have success
Wherever you go.

~ Sandy

NOTES

Introduction
1. Os Guinness, *The Call*, (Nashville, TN: Thomas Nelson, 2003), 81
2. CT Interview, "What Preparation Do Ministers Need Today? The Prerequisites of Pastoral Leadership." *CT Pastors,* Fall 2013. Retrieved from http://www.christianitytoday.com/pastors/2013/fall/what-preparation-do-ministers-need-today.html.
3. Nik Ripken, *The Insanity of God*, (Nashville: B&H Publishing Group, 2013), 32.
4. Bruce Gerencser, "21 Essential Tips for Young Pastors," *ExPastors*, www.expastors.com/advice-to-young-pastors/.

Chapter 1—The Greatest Battle of All—Faith
1. H.G. Wells, *War of the Worlds*, (New York: Penguin Group, 2005), 7.
2. Ron Walters, *Letters to Pastors* (United States: Xulonpress, 2008), 80.
3. James Ciment, editor, *Table of contents for Social issues in America: An Encyclopedia*, (Armonk, NY; M.E. Sharpe, 2006), http://catdir.loc.gov/catdir/toc/ecip0516/2005018778.html.
4. Sabrina Travernise, "U.S. Suicide Rate Surges to a 30-Year High," *New York Times*, April 22, 2016, http://www.nytimes.com/2016/04/22/health/us-suicide-rate-surges-to-a-30-year-high.html.

5. Sabrina Travernise, "Young Adolescence as Likely to Die from Suicide as from Traffic Accidents," *New York Times*, November 3, 2016, http://www.nytimes.com/2016/11/04/health/suicide-adolescents-traffic-deaths.html.
6. Sharon E. Watkins, "Racism Is Poisoning Our Society," *Time Magazine*, May 1, 2015, http://time.com/3843203/racism-is-poisoning-our-society/.
7. William Manchester and Paul Reid, *The Last Lion; Winston Spencer Churchill, Defender of the Realm 1940–1965*. (New York: Bantam Books, 2013), 182.
8. Paul McKay, "Jitterbugging for Jesus," Jan, 22, 2010, https://jitterbuggingforjesus.com/2010/01/22/a-brief-word-from-the-greatest-do-gooder-methodist-of-all-time-who-was-never-a-methodist/n.
9. Martin Luther, "A Mighty Fortress is Our God," *The Baptist Hymnal* (Nashville, TN: Convention Press, 1991), 8.
10. Francis J Crosby, Rescue the Perishing, 1869, https://www.umcdiscipleship.org/resources/history-of-hymns-rescue-the-perishing-crosby.
11. Thomas G. Long, "The Absurd in Worship," *The Christian Century*, Aug 13, 2012.

Chapter 2: The Deep Darkness—Doubts and Fears

1. Arthur W. Lindsley, Ph.D., Senior Fellow, "C.S. Lewis on Grief, Knowing & Doing,"*C.S. Lewis Institute*, Winter 2001, 3., http://www.cslewisinstitute.org/CS_Lewis_on_Grief_page3.
2. Richard Rodriguez, "Mother Teresa's Struggles with Faith," PBS News Hour, October 4, 2007. http://www.pbs.org/newshour/bb/religion-july-dec07-teresa_10-04/.
3. Philip Yancy, *Where is God When It Hurts* (Grand Rapids, MI: Zondervan, 1990), 168–169.
4. Catherine Marshall, *Meeting God at Every Turn*, (Lincoln, (Virginia: Chosen Books, 1980), xii.
5. Ibid.

Chapter 3: The Heart of the Problem—Sin

1. John Ortberg, "Dallas Willard, a Man from Another 'Time Zone," *Christianity Today*, May 8, 2013, http://www.christianitytoday.com/ct/2013/may-web-only/man-from-another-time-zone.html.
2. Os Guinness, *Impossible People* (Downers Grove, Illinois: IVP Books, 2016), 81,135.
3. C.S. Lewis, *The Problem of Pain* (San Francisco: Harper-Collins, 1940), 52,130.
4. Aldous Huxley, *Ends and Means* (New York, NY: Harper & Brothers, 1937), 270.
5. *Fanny and Alexander* (1982), http://www.rszoniq.com/the-bergman-suite/.
6. T.S. Eliot, "The Waste Land," http://www.bartleby.com/201/1.html.
7. Charles Hadden Spurgeon, Sermon 1546. Men Bewitched, *Spurgeon's Sermons Volume 26,* 1880.
8. Ralph Turnbull, editor, *The Best of D.L. Moody* (Grand Rapids, Michigan: Baker Books,1981), 31.
9. Dik and Chris Browne, *Hagar the Horrible*, 1973.

Chapter 4—The Remedy for Broken People in a Broken World—Grace

1. Sophie McDonalds, "When Fears Come True: The Corrie Ten Boom Story," *Reflecting the Son*, Mar 11, 2016, retrieved from https://sophiemcdonald.wordpress.com/2016/03/11/when-fears-come-true-the-corrie-ten-boom-story/.
2. Os Guinness, *The Call* (Nashville, TN: Thomas Nelson, 2003), 71.
3. John Bunyan, *Grace Abounding to the Chief of Sinners,* (London: George Larkin, 1666), 48, http://www.chapellibrary.org/files/4813/7642/2821/bun-abounding.pdf.
4. Brennan Manning, *All is Grace: A Ragamuffin Memoir* (Colorado Springs, CO: David C. Cook, 2011), 193–94.

5. Oswald Chambers, "By the Grace of God I Am What I Am" (Nov 16, 2016), *My Utmost for His Highest,* https://utmost.org/by-the-grace-of-god-i-am-what-i-am/.
6. Jonathan Edwards, "Glorious Grace," http://www.biblebb.com/files/edwards/gloriousgrace.htm.
7. C.S. Lewis, *The Inspirational Writings of C.S. Lewis: Surprised by Joy* (New York, NY: Inspirational Press, 1994), 125.

Chapter 5—The Toughest Job of All—Ministry

1. Malcolm Muggeridge, *"A twentieth century testimony",* (Thomas Nelson, 1978). http://www.azquotes.com/author/10521-Malcolm_Muggeridge.
2. Dennis N.T. Perkins, *Leading at the Edge,* (New York, NY: AMACOM, 2000), 2.
3. Charles Noel Douglas, *Forty Thousand Quotations: Prose and Poetical* (New York: Halcyon House, 1917), http://www.bartleby.com/348/.
4. Paul Tripp, "Dangerous Calling: Pastoral Ministry Is War," *The Christian Post,* 2016, http://www.christianpost.com/news/dangerous-calling-pastoral-ministry-is-war-74552/.
5. D. Martyn Lloyd-Jones, *Preachers and Preaching,* (Grand Rapids, Michigan: Zondervan, 1971), 105.
6. Philip Wagner, "The Secret Pain of Pastors," *Church Leaders,* Aug 29, 2014, https://churchleaders.com/pastors/pastor-articles/167379-philip-wagner-secret-pain-of-pastors.html/4.
7. Rev. A.B Simpson, *The Holy Spirit or the Power from on High* (New York: The Christian and Missionary Alliance Publishing Co., 1895), 107.
8. Bust Halo: Faith Shared Joyfully, *Daily Jolt,* Sept 5, 2011, http://bustedhalo.com/dailyjolt/sometimes-i-lie-awake-at-night-and-i-ask-where-have-i-gone-wrong-then-a-voice-says-to-me-this-is-going-to-take-more-than-one-night.
9. C.H. Spurgeon, *Lectures to My Students,* (Grand Rapids, Michigan: Zondervan, reprint 1979), 154.

10. Lain Murray, "Jonathan Edwards: The Life, the Man, and the Legacy," *Desiring God 2003 National Conference*, Oct 11, 2003, http://www.desiringgod.org/messages/jonathan-edwards-the-life-the-man-and-the-legacy.
11. Chris Armstrong, "Preacher in the Hands of an Angry Church: The Fall of Jonathan Edwards," *Grateful to the Dead: A Church Historian's Playground*. Dec 7, 2009. https://gratefultothedead.wordpress.com/2009/12/07/preacher-in-the-hands-of-an-angry-church-the-fall-of-jonathan-edwards/.
12. Mark Buchanan, "How I Got a Rhino Hide," *Leadership Journal.Net* (Winter 2016), 78.
13. Os Guinness, *The Call*, ((Nashville, TN: Thomas Nelson, 1998), 4.
14. Isaac Watts, *When I Surveyed the Wondrous Cross*, 1718.
15. Richard Rohr, "Transforming our Pain," *The Center for Action and Contemplation*, February 26, 2016, https://cac.org/transforming-our-pain-2016-02-26/.
16. J. Oswald Sanders, *Spiritual Leadership*, (Chicago: Moody Press, 1980), 223–234.

Chapter 6—The Altar of Strange Sacrifice—Marriage & Family

1. Magan Hill, "A Pastor is Not Married to the Church," *The Gospel Coalition*, Feb 12, 2016, https://www.thegospelcoalition.org/article/a-pastor-is-not-married-to-the-church.
2. Brian Croft, "10 habits to help a pastor stay married and in ministry," *The Southern Blog*, (The Southern Baptist Theological Seminary), December 6, 2016, http://www.sbts.edu/blogs/2016/12/06/10-habits-help-pastor-stay-married-ministry/.
3. Thomas Gray, "Elegy Written in a Country Churchyard," Thomas Gray Archives, London, 1751, Line 73, http://www.thomasgray.org/cgi-bin/display.cgi?text=elcc.

4. Bob Burns, Tasha D. Chapman, and Donald C. Guthrie, "Is Ministry Killing your Marriage?" *CT Pastors*, April 2013, http://www.christianitytoday.com/pastors/2013/april-online-only/is-ministry-killing-your-marriage.html.
5. Ibid.
6. Kara Miller, "What It Takes to Thrive in Ministry," *Christianity Today Weekly*, Jan 25, 2017, http://www.christianitytoday.com/lyris/eblast/archives/2017/ctweekly-semguide-012517.html.
7. Ibid.
8. Joe McKeever, "Why You May Not Want to Marry a Preacher," *Charisma News*, Oct 10, 2015, https://www.charismanews.com/opinion/52510-why-you-may-not-want-to-marry-a-preacher.
9. Bob Smietana, "Bill Hybels Resigns from Willow Creek," *Christianity Today*, April 10, 2018, https://www.christianitytoday.com/news/2018/april/bill-hybels-resigns-willow-creek-misconduct-allegations.html.
10. Bill Hybels, "The Character Crisis," *Preaching Today*, Tape No. 57.
11. Scott Cochran, "How to Keep 'Family First' in Ministry"—Bill Hybels, Oct 31, 2013, http://www.scottcochrane.com/index.php/2013/10/31/how-to-keep-family-first-in-ministry-bill-hybels/.

Chapter 7—THE SEARCH FOR AUTHENTICITY—IDENTITY

1. Op. cite, Gerencser
2. Adele Berlin and March Zvi Brettler, editors, *The Jewish Study Bible, TANAKH Translation* (New York, NY: Oxford University Press, 2004),111.
3. Denver C. Snuffer, Jr., Dwight Lyman Moody, *The 500th Anniversary of the Reformation*, Jan 9, 2017, https://www.christianreformation500years.info/dwight-lyman-moody.html.
4. Dietrich Bonhoeffer, *Letters and Papers From Prison*, edited by Eberhard Bethge, (New York: The Macmillan Company, 1959), 166, https://archive.org/stream/DietrichBonhoefferLettersFromPrison/Dietrich_Bonhoeffer_Letters_from_Prison_djvu.txt.

NOTES

5. Anne-Marie Alger, "'I don't know who I am anymore': Losing my identity," *Counselling Directory*, June 12, 2014. https://www.counselling-directory.org.uk/counsellor-articles/i-dont-know-who-i-am-anymore-losing-my-identity.
6. Bob Morrison, Patti Ryan, and Wanda Mallette, "Lookin' for Love," Sony/ATV Music Publishing LLC, released 1980.
7. Lisa Cannon Green, "Former Pastors Report Lack of Support Led to Abandoning Pastorate," LifeWay Research, January 12, 2016, Retrieved from https://lifewayresearch.com/2016/01/12/former-pastors-report-lack-of-support-led-to-abandoning-pastorate/.
8. Dennis P. Hollinger, "President's Report," *Annual Report 2017: For the Glory of God*, Gordon-Conwell Theological Seminary, 1
9. Green, op. cite., Ed Stetzer, holds the Billy Graham Chair of Church, Mission, and Evangelism at Wheaton College and serves as Executive Director of the Billy Graham Center.
10. Paul Tripp, "Your Identity is Not Your Ministry," *The Gospel Coalition*, U.S. Edition, May 13, 2012, https://www.thegospelcoalition.org/article/your-ministry-is-not-your-identity/.
11. C.S. Lewis, *Mere Christianity* (New York: Touchstone, a division of Simon & Schuster, 1996), 190.
12. Justin Paul and Benj Pasek, "This is Me" (lyrics), *The Greatest Showman*, Sony/ATV Music Publishing LLC, Kobalt Music Publishing Ltd., 2018.

Chapter 8—THE SURPRISE OF MINISTRY—JOY

1. Eugene H. Peterson, *The Contemplative Pastor* (Grand Rapids, Michigan: William B. Eerdmans), 63.
2. Paul David Tripp, *Instruments in the Redeemer's Hands* (Phillipsburg, New Jersey: P&R Publishing, 2002), 185–186.
3. D.L. Mayfield, *Assimilate or Go Home: Notes from a Failed Missionary on Rediscovering Faith* (New York, NY: HarperCollins, 2016) 199–201.

4. Carol Howard Merritt, "Ten reasons why being a pastor is the best job ever," *The Christian Century*, February 20, 2014. Retrieved from https://www.christiancentury.org/blogs/archive/2014-02/ten-reasons-why-being-pastor-best-job-ever.irr.
5. John Piper, "Joy in Christ Kept Him in China 1832–1905," June 4, 2018, Desiring God, https://www.desiringgod.org/articles/joy-in-christ-kept-him-in-china.
6. John Piper, "The Ministry of Hudson Taylor as Life in Christ," Feb. 5, 2014, Desiring God 2014 Conference for Pastors, https://www.desiringgod.org/messages/the-ministry-of-hudson-taylor-as-life-in-christ.
7. Elisha A. Hoffman, "Leaning on the Everlasting Arms," 1887, https://hymnary.org/text/what_a_fellowship_what_a_joy_divine.
8. David Nasser and Brent Crowe, *The Call* (United States: Redemptive Art Publishing, 2009), 115.
9. Public Domain, "The Story Behind the Heavenly Vision" (Turn Your Eyes Upon Jesus), Godtube, https://www.godtube.com/popular-hymns/the-heavenly-vision-turn-your-eyes-upon-jesus-/.
10. Miriam Rockness, "Reflections on the Art and Writings of Lilias Trotter," Retrieved from https://ililiastrotter.wordpress.com/about.

Chapter 9—THE CALL TO DUTY AND RESPONSIBILITY—THE CHARGE

1. John Styles, *The Life of David Brainerd with An Abridgement of His Diary and Journal*, (Boston: Samuel T. Armstrong and Crocker & Brewster, 1821), 188.
2. Phillip P. Bliss, "Wonderful Words of Life," 1874, Public Doman, *Timeless Truths*, https://library.timelesstruths.org/music/Wonderful_Words_of_Life/
3. Mandy Arthur, "Countdown: Greatest Quotes From The Legendary Vince Lombardi," *Success Fast Lane*, Sept 20, 2017, http://successfastlane.

NOTES

com/2017/09/30/countdown-greatest-quotes-from-the-legendary-vince-lombardi/.

4. Ibid.
5. Author unknown, possibly Coleman Cox, a humorist who compiled a collection of quotes. He authored *Take It from Me* and *Listen to This* (1922). https://quoteinvestigator.com/2012/07/21/luck-hard-work/ .
6. The Nation, "Unsinkable Hyman Rickover," *Time Magazine*, May 23, 1977 http://www.time.com/time/magazine/article/0,9171,911955,00.html.
7. Winston Churchill, "The Gift of a Common Tongue," Sept 6, 1943, International Churchill Society, https://winstonchurchill.org/resources/speeches/1941-1945-war-leader/the-price-of-greatness-is-responsibility/.
8. David J. Fant Jr, *A.W. Tozer: A Twentieth-Century Prophet*, (Chicago, Illinois: WingSpread, 2010), Chapter 1.
9. Arabella K. Hankey, "I Love to Tell the Story" (1866), *The Baptist Hymnal* (Nashville, TN: Convention Press, 1991), 572.
10. Arthur Owen Barfield, *The Inspiration Writings of C.S. Lewis*, (New York, NY: Inspirational Press, 1994), p. 125.

www.ingramcontent.com/pod-product-compliance
Lightning Source LLC
Chambersburg PA
CBHW051106160426
43193CB00010B/1343